*sparkteach

TEACHING THE CLASSICS TO TODAY'S STUDENTS

Much Ado About Nothing

WILLIAM SHAKESPEARE

*sparknotes FOR TEACHERS™

*sparkteach

ISBN 978-1-4114-8004-9

Distributed in Canada by Sterling Publishing Co., Inc.
C/o Canadian Manda Group, 664 Annette Street
Toronto, Ontario M6S 2C8, Canada
Distributed in the United Kingdom by GMC Distribution Services
Castle Place, 166 High Street, Lewes, East Sussex BN7 1XU, England
Distributed in Australia by NewSouth Books
University of New South Wales, Sydney, NSW 2052, Australia

For information about custom editions, special sales, and premium
and corporate purchases, please contact Sterling Special Sales
at 800-805-5489 or specialsales@sterlingpublishing.com.

Manufactured in Canada

2 4 6 8 10 9 7 5 3 1

sparkteach.com
sparknotes.com
sterlingpublishing.com

Cover design by Elizabeth Mihaltse Lindy
Cover and title page illustration by MUTI
Interior design by Kevin Ullrich
Image credits: Courtesy of the Cleveland Museum of Art: 63; Getty Images: filborg/
iStock/Getty Images Plus: 14, 15; Courtesy of the Metropolitan Museum of Art: 62 top;
Shutterstock.com: Gimas: 45; Courtesy of Wikimedia Commons: 62 bottom; Geni: 61

Contents

PART 1

Welcome to SparkTeach!

SparkTeach is a unique set of teaching guides and lesson plans designed to help make classic literature engaging and relevant to today's students.

We asked teachers about the biggest challenges they face in their English classes, and their answer was clear: "We need to engage our students, spark their interest in literature, and make our lessons relevant." That's why we developed SparkTeach, customizable materials including teaching frameworks, lessons, in-class worksheets, and more for the most popular titles taught today!

The following pages provide you with helpful tips for lesson planning and classroom management, an explanation of each component, including a detailed description of a "Real-Life Lens Lesson"; an explanation of the role of the ELA Common Core State Standards in the program; and guidelines for student assessment.

SparkTeach materials are easily customizable and can be adapted for many different learning styles. We encourage you to utilize the lessons as best fits your classroom's needs.

Tips for Class Planning and Management

Here are some tips for planning and managing your class as students work their way through a SparkTeach unit. To maximize student learning and engagement:

1. Preview SparkTeach Materials

Review all the materials available for a text. Decide which worksheets you will use based on student needs. You may choose materials to match a particular text in your curriculum, or you may assign a text after being inspired by a specific Real-Life Lens Lesson.

2. Gather Your Materials

Once you've selected the components you'll need, preview each lesson and then download and print all of the chosen worksheets. Be sure to print out enough copies for each student and one copy for yourself to use as reference. Hand out all worksheets needed prior to reading, such as Contextual Support Handouts, as these promote student comprehension.

If the Real-Life Lens Lesson or Film Lesson requires a specific film, make sure to have the film on hand to show the class. If specific scene timestamps are provided, preview the scenes so that you will feel prepared to answer students' questions.

Review the Midpoint Activities and Final Project options in the Real-Life Lens Lesson. Will you need specific equipment such as a video recorder or a printer for students to complete a project? Be sure your students will have access to the tools they'll need to complete their work.

3. Set Your Schedule

Once you've chosen a Real-Life Lens Lesson, read it through before starting. Choose your start, midpoint, and end dates to keep on schedule. Each framework should take multiple class periods to complete; plan each activity and project accordingly. Will students need access to the school library or the internet to conduct research for their final projects? If so, be sure to schedule time for student research, review, and revision.

4. Preview Real-Life Links

Read, watch, or listen to each of the Real-Life Links. Decide which resources will engage your students the most. Prepare a few questions to use to ignite student thinking, guide quick written responses, and initiate class discussion.

5. Monitor Student Progress and Comprehension

Routinely schedule one-on-one meetings with students to check their comprehension and progress throughout reading. During group work or discussions, circulate around the room to monitor student collaboration and communication and to gently guide discussions back on topic, if necessary. Recording your observations and assessments will enable you to note individual and whole-class progress as work continues.

6. Let Students Shine

Schedule plenty of time for all students to present their final projects. They have worked hard all month, and showing off their finished work boosts confidence and allows students to see the unique and creative ways their peers interpreted and approached a similar topic.

7. Personalize Content

Real-Life Lens Lessons are designed to ensure students engage with each text in a meaningful way. Lenses are specially chosen to help students connect with even the most challenging texts on a personal level. As you progress through the materials, look for ways to help students relate the text to their own lives. Notice what excites them and tailor your lessons accordingly.

What's Included in SparkTeach?

Real-Life Lens Lessons

The Real-Life Lens Lesson is a unit that focuses on a specific text over multiple class periods. The driving force behind each unit is the lens, a carefully selected theme through which students view the text. This lens provides students with a relatable point of entry. A thorough explanation of each feature in a Real-Life Lens Lesson is detailed in the next section beginning on page 8. Each Real-Life Lens Lesson includes several reproducible worksheets and assessment materials to round out the unit.

Reading Skills Worksheets

Each set of teaching materials features multiple Reading Skills Worksheets designed to help develop the ELA reading skills outlined in the Common Core State Standards. Worksheets engage students in a variety of activities that deepen understanding of both the skill and the featured text. Each worksheet is reproducible.

Vocabulary Builders

Each set of teaching materials also includes at least one Vocabulary Builder based on the specific language found in the text. You can pass out the builder prior to starting the text and refer to it as students read to ensure comprehension. Other builders ask students to engage with the vocabulary through graphic organizers, charts, or other activities. Each builder is reproducible.

Contextual Support Handouts

To aid comprehension, each set of teaching materials features at least one Contextual Support handout to provide information to students about topics relevant to the text. Student comprehension is hindered if historical or background information is unknown or not clear. We developed these handouts to arm students with the information they'll need to better understand each text.

Poetics Lessons

Understanding poetic devices helps students comprehend classic and modern texts and appreciate a writer's choices and craft. Each poetics lesson provides an in-depth exploration of a key poetic device, such as metaphor or simile. Each lesson features examples from the literary text that demonstrate the topic and provides a foundation from which students can work. These lessons come with reproducible student-facing worksheets and sample answers.

Film Lessons

When teaching Shakespeare, it's good to remember that the works were intended to be acted out by players and viewed by an audience, not read as literature. Students can benefit greatly and process these texts most effectively by experiencing Shakespeare's plays visually. Film productions of Shakespeare's plays provide a wealth of learning opportunities. We designed SparkTeach Film Lessons to help connect Shakespearean texts with a modern audience and help students—especially visual learners—engage with the texts in a new way. These lessons also allow for more differentiation in the classroom and deepen students' understanding of the plays. Each lesson comes with reproducible student-facing worksheets and sample answers.

What Makes Real-Life Lens Lessons Unique?

Real-Life Lens Lessons, the hub of SparkTeach materials, set this literature program apart. Each Real-Life Lens Lesson is thoughtfully designed to help students view the text—even older or more challenging works—through a relatable lens that enables students to connect with the text in a meaningful way. A powerful teaching tool, each teacher-facing Real-Life Lens Lesson provides a framework for organizing and executing a unit over multiple class periods that focuses on a particular work of literature. Each element found in a Real-Life Lens Lesson is listed and described below.

1. The Lens

The lens is the heart of each Real-Life Lens Lesson. The lens shapes classroom discussions, student analysis, and all lesson activities and projects. The lens invites students to explore the text in a way that connects the content with their own lives—their experiences, concerns, interests, and aspirations.

Introduce the Lens Through Real-Life Links

- Each Real-Life Lens Lesson features several Real-Life Links including online articles, podcasts, videos, and surveys.

- Real-Life Links are meant to be shared with students prior to or during reading.

- After students read, listen to, or watch the Real-Life Links, but before reading of the text begins, the class participates in an activity designed to introduce the lens to students in a meaningful way.

2. Big Idea Questions

- The Big Idea Questions are overarching questions that provide students with a base from which to start thinking about the text. For example: "Is it ever okay to dupe or tell lies to someone you care about?" (See page 15.)

- Students are encouraged to return to these questions as they read and note how their answers to the questions change over the course of the unit.

3. Driving Questions

In addition to the Big Idea Questions, each Real-Life Lens Lesson contains a number of Driving Questions. Unlike the Big Idea Questions, Driving Questions are more specific in their focus and are designed to guide student exploration of the text, as related to the lens. Some examples of Driving Questions featured in *Much Ado About Nothing* include:

- Does Don Pedro need to wear a disguise and pretend to be Claudio to woo Hero for his friend? Why can't Claudio woo her himself?

- Why does Don Pedro decide that Beatrice and Benedick should fall in love with one another, and how does he propose to make this happen?

- Don John resolves to play tricks to interfere in Hero and Claudio's relationship. What motivates Don John?

4. Differentiated Instruction

- To ensure all students can access learning, we have provided differentiated instruction for all Midpoint Activities and final projects.

- Suggestions for increasing and/or decreasing the difficulty of each activity and project are found throughout each Real-Life Lens Lesson.

5. Midpoint Activities

- Two engaging Midpoint Activities are featured to ensure student comprehension of the text and give you an opportunity to assess learning.

- These activities encourage students to consolidate their understanding of the text so far and challenge them to use that understanding to make predictions about the rest of the text and analyze what they know of the plot, characters, or theme.

6. Paired Text Recommendations

- Our list of paired text recommendations suggests contemporary works you can pair with the classic work you're teaching.

- Students can connect to passages from multiple works by comparing, contrasting, and analyzing the works side by side.

7. Final Projects

- Each Real-Life Lens Lesson presents students with two options for final projects that encapsulate what they have learned about the text as seen through the lens.

- Students are invited to choose the project that excites them the most at the beginning of the unit and to keep this project in mind as they read.

- These dynamic projects are designed to provide opportunities for students to demonstrate their mastery of the text in creative and fun ways.

- Examples of projects include creating a multimedia presentation or video, rewriting and performing a scene from the text, and participating in a formal debate on a specific issue.

8. Supporting Worksheets and Graphic Organizers

- Each Real-Life Lens Lesson offers several reproducible worksheets, including a **Driving Questions Worksheet, located on page 87,** on which students can record answers as they read, and graphic organizers to support student learning.

- To save you time and help students understand how to tackle each task, each worksheet includes scaffolded directions and a sample student response if necessary.

9. Student and Teacher Reflection Worksheets

- The **Student Reflection Worksheet, located on page 102,** encourages students to assess their strengths, weaknesses, and level of engagement throughout the Real-Life Lens Lesson.

- Self-assessment cultivates confidence, as students note how they worked through challenges; nurtures good study habits; and encourages students to take responsibility for their own learning.

- The **Teacher Reflection Worksheet, located on page 103,** allows you to evaluate what elements of the unit students found the most engaging, where they seemed to struggle, and what approaches or elements worked the best for you and your class.

SparkTeach and the Common Core State Standards

Every component included in SparkTeach was developed to ensure broad coverage of the ELA Common Core State Standards. Materials were designed to provide multiple opportunities for your students to address a wide variety of Reading Literature, Speaking and Listening, Writing, and Language standards.

Each standard addressed by an activity, discussion, or project is listed for easy reference so that you can track which standards each lesson or worksheet covers.

Guidelines for Student Assessment

Each set of SparkTeach materials provides extensive assessment opportunities, including a **Rubric for Student Assessment, a Student Reflection Worksheet, and a Teacher Reflection Worksheet (see pages 98–103)**. Use these assets, along with lesson-specific assessment advice within each Real-Life Lens Lesson, to successfully gauge student learning.

Worksheet Assessment

Many Reading Skills Worksheets and Vocabulary Builders may be scored in a traditional fashion. To make grading easier and faster, we have provided full answer keys for worksheets that contain clear correct or incorrect answers and sample student answers for worksheets that require more subjective, open-ended answers.

Real-Life Lens Lesson Assessment

Each Real-Life Lens Lesson offers opportunities for informal, formal, and self-assessment. Performance assessment involves observing student collaboration, while formal assessment entails grading a writing assignment, worksheet, or final project.

SparkTeach
Much Ado About Nothing
Lesson Plans

Real-Life Lens Lesson
Tricks and Lies

Use this Real-Life Lens Lesson to help students dive deep into Shakespeare's *Much Ado About Nothing* and examine the play's language, characters, and plot devices through the lens of tricks and lies. Why do people play tricks and games on others? Do most relationships begin with complete honesty? What makes a lie convincing? Why are some people more gullible than others?

Materials

Much Ado About Nothing by William Shakespeare

Worksheets: Driving Questions, page 87
The Path of True Love, page 89

Introduce the Lens

To activate students' thinking, choose one or two of the following Real-Life Links to use in an engagement activity. Have students read or watch the material and discuss the content. Encourage students to jot down notes, or record class notes on the board for future reference.

Real-Life Links: Tricks and Relationships

What Teens Think About: Healthy Relationships
This myHealth short video features teens talking about what they consider to be a good romantic relationship.

https://rb.gy/g1lk8v

From Eye Contact to Aloofness, 4 Techniques to Make Him Fall in Love with You
In this *Today* article, relationship expert Tracey Cox shares four techniques, based on science, to make someone fall for you.

https://rb.gy/gf0dub

White Lies: Kind or Cruel?

In this *Psychology Today* article, psychologist Jennifer Lea Reynolds debates the pros and cons of telling little lies in a relationship.

https://rb.gy/hm0ieq

Teen Voices: Dating in the Digital Age

This article from the Pew Research Center shares the results of teen focus groups on how social media impacts romantic relationships and features quotes that discuss some of the games and tricks people use, such as liking tweets or ignoring a text.

https://rb.gy/oiekys

Pose the Following Big Idea Questions to the Class:

Why do people tell white lies or play tricks to get someone to like them? Are tricks and lies necessary?
Is it ever okay to dupe or tell lies to someone you care about?

Engagement Activity

- Have students reflect on their own relationships or relationships in films or books to write quick initial answers to the questions.

- Have them discuss the questions in small groups.

- Instruct students to decide as a group if relationships can ever be completely straightforward and honest. After groups have concluded their discussions and decided "yes" or "no," have them share their ideas and conclusions with the class.

- Following discussion, give students time to revise their initial responses.

CCSS: SL.11-12.1

Introduce the Driving Questions

Begin by having students write their own questions about the lesson topic. Encourage them to think about what they already know about playing tricks and/or telling lies in relationships and what they are interested in exploring further.

Hand out the **Driving Questions Worksheet, located on page 87**. Review the questions as a class. Students should enter initial answers to the questions as they read *Much Ado About Nothing*. They will revisit the questions and revise their answers following the lesson activities, classroom discussion, and completion of the text. Remind students to support their responses with text evidence.

Integrate the Driving Questions into your classroom discussions. Use them to help guide students' thinking about the Big Idea Questions.

1. Does Don Pedro need to wear a disguise and pretend to be Claudio to woo Hero for his friend? Why can't Claudio woo her himself?
2. Why does Don Pedro decide that Beatrice and Benedick should fall in love with one another, and how does he propose to make this happen?
3. Don John resolves to play tricks to interfere in Hero and Claudio's relationship. What motivates Don John?
4. What tricks and lies does Don Pedro use to make Benedick believe that Beatrice loves him?
5. What tricks and lies does Hero use to make Beatrice believe that Benedick loves her?
6. What are the serious ramifications of the trick that Don John plays on Claudio regarding Hero?
7. What is the lie the friar suggests telling about Hero? How does he expect the lie will uncover the truth and clear Hero's good name?
8. How does the wedding scene rely on tricks and lies?

> **CCSS: RL.11-12.1**

Introduce the "Through the Lens" Activity

Activity: Tricks and Lies in Romance

In this activity, students will discuss the many different ways people play games and tell little lies in order to make their crush interested in them.

Ask students a series of questions and have them raise their hands if they agree:

- Do you know anyone who has ever played "hard to get," for instance, by ignoring a text from his or her crush?

- Do you know anyone who has "liked" a social media post to express interest in the person who posted it?

- Do you know anyone who has pretended they liked a band or a sport because his or her crush liked it?

- Do you know anyone who has pretended to ignore someone he or she had a crush on?

- Do you know anyone who has pretended to like someone else to make a crush jealous?

- Do you know anyone who has ever lied about someone's appearance to make that person happy?

Go through the questions quickly so students can see how prevalent playing games and telling white lies are in relationships. When you have completed the list, ask students if these tricks and lies generally worked by asking: *Did the person get his or her crush to like him or her back?* Invite students to share the results of the situations they know about with the class.

Organize students into small groups and have them discuss what it would be like if, instead of playing games, people were completely honest in relationships. As an example, tell students to imagine he or she just got a text from a crush and responded *immediately*. Ask students: *What would the crush think? Would the crush be pleased or scared away?*

Have students share and discuss a few more examples within their groups. Then have them write a paragraph sharing their opinion about whether playing tricks and telling little lies is helpful in developing relationships or whether it's harmful. Invite volunteers to share their paragraphs with the class.

CCSS: SL.11-12.1, W.11-12.1

Differentiated Instruction

This activity can be modified to help all students access learning.

Decrease Difficulty

Instead of having students write a paragraph, each group will simply decide if playing tricks and telling lies is helpful in a relationship. Then take a quick class poll.

Increase Difficulty

Instead of individuals writing a paragraph, each group will write a short script that shows how tricks and lies are used by people in relationships as well as the effects of these tricks and lies, either positive or negative. Groups can perform their scripts if you like.

Introduce the Final Project

Before moving on, introduce the final projects to the class (page 20). Have students choose the project they will complete and encourage them to keep their project in mind as they read the text. Facilitate the formation of project groups if necessary.

Assign the Midpoint Activities

Activity 1: Beatrice and Benedick

After finishing Act 3, scene 1, students will pause their reading to analyze the efforts characters have made to trick Beatrice and Benedick into falling in love. Students will

- Find and cite a list of at least three places in the text that describe the plot to bring the pair together, including Don Pedro's plan, Hero and Claudio's participation, and the results of the trick.

- Evaluate and make a list of reasons why Don Pedro, Hero, and Claudio are willing to tell lies to get Beatrice and Benedick together, and why they think Don Pedro's trick will work.

- To facilitate student thinking, ask questions such as: *Do Beatrice and Benedick seem right for each other? Why would they have to be tricked into falling in love in the first place?*

- Organize students with partners to share their lists and discuss whether they think Beatrice and Benedick make a good couple. Have pairs share their thoughts with the class.

CCSS: RL.11-12.1, SL.11-12.1, W.11-12.3, W.11-12.4

Differentiated Instruction

Decrease Difficulty

Draw the following chart on the board that students can copy in their notebooks and use to evaluate Beatrice and Benedick's compatibility:

	Yes	Somewhat	No
Do Beatrice and Benedick have similar personalities?			
Is there evidence of a prior relationship between them?			
Do Beatrice and Benedick seem to get along?			
Do their friends and family think they are compatible?			

If students have difficulty finding scenes in the play to help answer the questions, guide them to Act 1, scene 2, in which Don Pedro introduces his plan, and Act 2, scene 3, in which the men, while telling lies about Beatrice's "feelings" for Benedick, still reveal truths about Beatrice's and Benedick's characters.

Increase Difficulty

Have students write a short scene in which Beatrice and Benedick share their new feelings of love for one another, mimicking their specific speech styles.

Activity 2: The Role of Tricks and Lies

After finishing Act 3, scene 3, students will pause their reading to analyze the role that tricks and lies play in the unfolding of the plots to bring Beatrice and Benedick together and to break Hero and Claudio apart.

Students will review the text, looking for the key events in both plot lines while paying particular attention to the tricks and lies that were employed. Have students use **The Path of True Love Worksheet, located on page 89,** to chart the development of the plots and the impact of tricks and lies.

Once students have completed their graphic organizers, organize them into small groups so they can discuss what they've read of the play so far. Ask students to predict what will happen to the pairs of lovers in the second half of the play. Have groups write down their predictions and the text evidence that supports their predictions on their worksheets or in their notebooks.

Differentiated Instruction

Decrease Difficulty

Before reviewing the text, work with the class to recall how the dual plots unfold. Ask questions such as: *Whose idea was it to make Beatrice and Benedick fall in love? What was the plan? What happened after the plan was introduced? Who initiated the plot to divide Hero and Claudio? What was the plan? What actions did this person take?* Write each chain of events on the board. Then organize students into small groups to find the text that supports each of these events and add more details. Students will complete their charts together and then proceed to discussion.

Increase Difficulty

Point out that before Claudio and Hero got engaged, Claudio believed Don Pedro was wooing Hero at the dance for himself. Have students create another graphic organizer showing the events and the tricks and lies that pertain to that subplot.

Paired Text Recommendations

Encourage students to read passages from contemporary works that similarly feature the theme of tricks and lies. In pairing multiple texts with similar themes, students are challenged to look beyond the work they're studying and find new ways to connect to the themes. Here are some works you can pair with *Much Ado About Nothing*:

- *The Only Thing Worse Than Me Is You* by Lily Anderson

- *Speak Easy, Speak Love* by McKelle George

- *Under a Dancing Star* by Laura Wood

Final Projects

Students will work on their final projects after they have finished reading the complete text of *Much Ado About Nothing*. Both projects call for small groups.

CCCS: RL.11-12.1, RL.11-12.3, RL.11-12.5, SL.11-12.1, SL.11-12.6, W.11-12.3, W.11-12.4

Final Project 1: Claudio in Love

Students will work in groups to come to a greater understanding of Claudio's character by analyzing his response to the tricks played on him and the lies told to him.

First, groups will find each instance in the text in which Claudio is tricked or lied to in his pursuit of love and then evaluate Claudio's reactions. Have students locate an important passage, cite the text, and write a short response to answer the following questions: *Does Claudio believe the trick or lie? Does he question what is happening? What does he learn from this experience, and how does it affect what happens next?* Remind students to include scenes with Claudio and scenes in which events pertaining to him are described by other characters.

Next, have groups re-read and discuss Claudio's words in Act 4, scene 1, in which he denounces Hero. Have them consider the following questions: *What is Claudio's main message here? Why is he behaving as he is? What does this speech reveal about Claudio's character?*

Have groups use their research thus far to come to an understanding of Claudio's strengths and weaknesses. Students can create lists, brainstorm adjectives, write a paragraph, or use other methods to organize their ideas.

Finally, groups will use their knowledge of Claudio's character to create three profiles of Claudio for a fictitious matchmaking website. Profiles should be written from the point of view of Claudio, Don John, and the students themselves. Remind groups that each profile should highlight the way the "writer" perceives Claudio; for instance, Claudio might see himself as "romantic," while Don John might perceive him as "gullible." Students can use web software, presentation software, or poster paper to create their profiles. Have groups share their profiles with the class, and have the listening students guess the viewpoint.

Differentiated Instruction

Decrease Difficulty

Provide the locations of some key scenes to analyze: Act 3, scene 2 (Claudio listens to Don John's slander and agrees to spy on Hero); Act 3, scene 3 (Borachio reports on Claudio's reaction to the scene in Hero's window); Act 5, scene 1 (Claudio finds out the truth and agrees to marry Hero's cousin); Act 5, scene 4 (Claudio marries the masked Hero).

Increase Difficulty

Have groups write short responses to one or more of Claudio's profiles as if they were one of the other characters in the play. Responses can be from any character but must draw upon that person's own temperament and personality. For instance, Beatrice would likely perceive Claudio as a man too weak to make a good match with her.

Final Project 2: A Dangerous Trick

Students will work in groups of five or six to study and understand how the trick Don John played on Claudio takes a serious turn after Hero is falsely and publicly denounced.

Groups will first perform a close reading of Act 4, scene 1, in which Claudio explains his reasons for refusing to marry Hero and then find and enumerate possible consequences of Claudio's accusation, both stated in the text (for example, Leonato killing Hero) and implied (for instance, Hero will become a social pariah).

Groups will focus on this dramatic twist, discussing what impact it has on the tone and message of the play and advancing hypotheses about why Shakespeare made the decision to include this twist. Remind students to consider events in Act 5 to inform their analyses. All students in a group should take notes on their discussion, keeping track of important points.

Groups will then use their analyses to write an alternate ending to the play, which can be in modern English, and act it out for the class. Each student should perform a different role.

Differentiated Instruction

Decrease Difficulty

Ask groups these questions to help them analyze the impact of Act 4, scene 1:

- What words would you use to describe the tone of the play up through Act 3? What words would you use to describe the tone of Claudio's accusation of Hero?

- What does Beatrice ask Benedick to do as a result of Claudio's accusation? What does Leonato say he is going to do? How do threats of violence upend the tone of the play?

- How does the tone of Act 4 compare with the tone of Act 5? Does Act 5 continue to build the somber mood of Act 4, or does it reverse that tone?

- What do you think Shakespeare's message was up through Act 3? What message does Shakespeare share in Act 4? What is his message in Act 5?

Increase Difficulty

Challenge students to write in imitation of Shakespeare instead of using modern English.

Assess the Assignments

Use the **Rubric for Student Assessment, located on page 99,** to evaluate student work on the lesson assignments.

Distribute the **Student Reflection Worksheet, located on page 102**. Guide students through the self-assessment and reflection questions.

Complete the **Teacher Reflection Worksheet, located on page 103**. Record which elements of the lesson plan worked well for your class and which elements you might revise for future classes.

Poetics Lesson
Prose in the Play

Lesson Overview

Students will define *prose* and *verse*, understand how the forms differ, and learn how to identify passages of each in William Shakespeare's *Much Ado About Nothing*. Students will understand that prose and verse are used to express different types of speech, situations, and emotional states. While this lesson can be completed at any time, note that cited examples could reveal plot points.

Materials

Much Ado About Nothing by William Shakespeare

Worksheet: Prose in the Play, page 91

Lesson Objectives

1. Students will understand how prose differs from verse in Shakespeare's plays and how to identify prose passages.
2. Students will learn why Shakespeare uses prose or verse for different speeches in *Much Ado About Nothing*.
3. Students will discuss and analyze examples of prose and verse in *Much Ado About Nothing*.

Instructional Sequence

1. Define *prose* and *verse* and examine the use of each in Shakespeare's plays.
William Shakespeare uses two different types of writing in his plays: prose and verse. Write the definitions of *prose* and *verse* on the board and review them with students.

> ***Prose*** **is a piece of writing that has no regular pattern of rhythm, or meter. Prose sounds like ordinary speech and appears on the written page in blocks of sentences that form a paragraph. Prose relies on literary devices to give it a sense of movement; in Shakespeare's writing, these include puns, lists, alliteration, and assonance.**

Verse is a piece of writing that has a set rhythm. Verse refers to a single line or group of lines that forms a poetic composition. When characters speak in verse, they are expressing themselves in poetry. Shakespeare usually wrote in blank verse, which means the lines have no rhyme scheme but do have a pattern of stressed and unstressed syllables.

Provide examples of prose and verse using short quotes from other Shakespeare plays with which students are familiar. This example comes from *Romeo and Juliet*. Write the prose and verse versions of the quote on the board and read aloud for students to hear how each sounds.

Verse: What's in a name? That which we call a rose / By any other word would smell as sweet. (*No Fear*: 2.2.43–44)

Prose: You can call a rose by a different name. It would still smell as sweet.

All of Shakespeare's plays contain a mixture of prose and verse. Tell students to be aware of the two forms as they read; not only do they sound different, but on the page, prose looks like a paragraph while verse looks like a poem.

2. Examine the language in *Much Ado About Nothing*.

Much Ado About Nothing contains the most prose of any of Shakespeare's plays—almost 75 percent of the play. In many of Shakespeare's plays, lower-status characters speak in prose while higher-born characters are more likely to speak in verse; however, *Much Ado About Nothing* does not follow these distinctions. Don Pedro, for example, speaks in both prose and verse.

Copy the following lines from *Much Ado About Nothing* on the board. Tell students that this exchange, written in prose, takes place between the high-status governor of Messina and a low-status messenger. The passage opens the play, setting the tone for equality of language among members of all social classes. Read the passage aloud.

LEONATO
I learn in this letter that Don Pedro of Aragon comes this
night to Messina.

MESSENGER
He is very near by this. He was three leagues off when
I left him.

LEONATO

How many gentlemen have you lost in this action?

MESSENGER

But few of any sort, and none of name.

LEONATO

A victory is twice itself when the achiever brings home full numbers. I find here that Don Pedro hath bestowed much honor on a young Florentine called Claudio.

(*No Fear*: 1.1.1–9)

Ask students: *Did this exchange sound like an ordinary conversation or like a poem?*

3. Explain that prose is the language of realism and wit.

Prose was considered a more practical, realistic form of language than verse; thus, it suits a play like *Much Ado About Nothing*, which mainly focuses on common daily concerns. Prose also serves Beatrice and Benedick well since they reject the fanfare of marriage in favor of agile verbal sparring. The quickness with which they riff off one another signifies their cleverness and ability at wordplay; thus prose also serves as the language of wit in *Much Ado About Nothing*.

Read the following aloud for students:

BEATRICE

Against my will, I am sent to bid you come in to dinner.

BENEDICK

Fair Beatrice. I thank you for your pains.

BEATRICE

I took no more pains for those thanks than you take pains to thank me. If it had been painful, I would not have come.

(*No Fear*: 2.3.206–209)

Ask students to provide a summary of the exchange. Then discuss how Beatrice seizes upon Benedick's use of the word *pains*, turning it back on him as an insult. Also point out that this conversation reflects eating a meal, which is a daily, practical matter.

Then, share this example from Beatrice:

BEATRICE

"Then" is spoken. Fare you well now. And yet, ere I go, let me go with that I came, which is, with knowing what hath passed between you and Claudio.

BENEDICK

Only foul words, and thereupon I will kiss thee.

BEATRICE

Foul words is but foul wind, and foul wind is but foul breath, and foul breath is noisome. Therefore I will depart unkissed.

(*No Fear*: 5.2.33–39)

After ensuring students' comprehension of the excerpt, ask what words are used repetitively and how this repetition makes the exchange humorous. Then ask them how this exchange signifies practical, realistic matters.

Beatrice and Benedick's quick wit also shines when they are speaking with others:

CLAUDIO

Benedick, didst thou note the daughter of Signior Leonato?

BENEDICK

I noted her not, but I looked on her.

(*No Fear*: 1.1.126–127)

In this exchange, Benedick makes a pun out of Claudio's words: Claudio uses *note* to mean "notice," but Benedick responds that he did not notice her—implying she (Hero) wasn't noteworthy—even though he looked at her.

Further, prose represents the language of logic as when Benedick muses over learning of Beatrice's supposed love for him:

BENEDICK

> This can be no trick. The conference was
> sadly borne; they have the truth of this from Hero; they
> seem to pity the lady. It seems her affections have their full
> bent. Love me? Why, it must be requited!
>
> (*No Fear*: 2.3.183–186)

Here, Benedick uses logic and reason to evaluate the news he has overheard. Beatrice must love him because his friends, who learned about it from the virtuous Hero, spoke earnestly. When he decides to return Beatrice's love, he is following his mind, not his heart.

Most of the characters speak in prose at various points in the play. This conversational tone helps drive the narrative, particularly in Acts 1 through 3, where little dramatic action takes place.

4. Explain that verse is the language of emotions and formalities.

When verse is used in *Much Ado About Nothing*, the language signifies strong emotion, formalities, and artifice. Copy this instance when Benedick speaks in verse on the board:

BENEDICK

> Your answer, sir, is enigmatical.
> But for my will, my will is your goodwill
> May stand with ours, this day to be conjoined
> In the state of honorable marriage—
> In which, good Friar, I shall desire your help.
>
> (*No Fear*: 5.4.27–31)

Put the text in context: Benedick is asking Leonato for permission to marry Beatrice. Discuss with students why in this serious moment, Benedick reverts to verse.

Then share Beatrice's reaction to overhearing that Benedick loves her:

BEATRICE

What fire is in mine ears? Can this be true?

Stand I condemned for pride and scorn so much?

Contempt, farewell, and maiden pride, adieu!

No glory lives behind the back of such.

And Benedick, love on; I will requite thee,

Taming my wild heart to thy loving hand.

If thou dost love, my kindness shall incite thee

To bind our loves up in a holy band.

For others say thou dost deserve, and I

Believe it better than reportingly.

(*No Fear*: 3.1.113–122)

Ask a volunteer to summarize Beatrice's soliloquy. Then discuss with students why Beatrice responds to this revelation in verse, while Benedick responds to a similar revelation in prose: Hearing that she is too full of pride, Beatrice reacts in an emotional, not logical, manner.

Ask: *What are the main differences between prose and verse?*

5. Give students a chance to apply and practice what they have learned.

Pass out the **Prose in the Play Worksheet, located on page 91,** and have students complete the worksheet individually or in pairs.

CCSS: RL.11-12.1, RL.11-12.4, RL.11-12.5

Differentiated Instruction

This activity can be modified to help all students access learning.

Decrease Difficulty

Provide ways to determine whether text is prose or verse. Encourage students to recite passages aloud, listening for a conversational sound or a poetic sound. Have them practice with one another or in small groups. Then, using the text, point out the visual clues that can help. In prose, the lines of text extend all the way to the page margin and are usually justified; the first letter of each line is often lowercase, just like in a sentence; and the lines do not all have the same number of syllables. In verse, the lines of text are usually shorter, and the first word of each line is capitalized regardless of standard rules of punctuation.

Increase Difficulty

Provide students a choice of these follow-up activities:

Some critics believe that prose is used in *Much Ado About Nothing* to show Beatrice and Benedick upending social norms. Have students consider this critical viewpoint, determine whether or not, and write a short response, justifying their point of view with textual examples.

In Act 2, scene 3, lines 16–19 (*No Fear* edition), Benedick says of Claudio:

> He was wont to speak plain and to the purpose
> like an honest man and a soldier, and now is he turned
> orthography; his words a very fantastical banquet, just
> so many strange dishes.

Have students analyze Benedick's explanation for Claudio's switch from prose to verse, and then find examples to determine if Benedick is correct.

Film Lesson

Through the Directors' Eyes

Directors face an enormous challenge when bringing any work of literature to the screen. Directors must make decisions regarding the physical aspects of the film, such as setting and costumes, and also decide what cinematic techniques to use. No two directors will make the same choices, but all directors who film Shakespeare recognize the unique responsibility of bringing the playwright's words to life.

The actor and director Kenneth Branagh transformed *Much Ado About Nothing* into a film in 1993 to great acclaim. Then, in 2012, Joss Whedon shot a new version of the play. How did each filmmaker bring his own vision to Shakespeare's creation?

In this lesson, students will explore the ways in which each director presents the same scene and how closely it hews to Shakespeare's own words. Students will also determine which film they believe brings the scene most to life.

For this assignment, students will reread Beatrice and Benedick's meeting in Act 1, scene 1, lines 93–114 (*No Fear* edition). Then, they will watch the same scene in the two directors' versions of *Much Ado About Nothing* several times in order to compare them. Finally, they will decide which version they think most accurately represents Shakespeare's intent and which version they prefer.

Materials

Much Ado About Nothing by William Shakespeare

Worksheet: Through the Directors' Eyes, page 94

Much Ado About Nothing directed by Kenneth Branagh, BBC Films, 1993
Much Ado About Nothing directed by Joss Whedon, Bellwether Pictures, 2012

Lesson Objectives

1. Students will reread the scene presenting Beatrice and Benedick's first encounter in *Much Ado About Nothing*.
2. Students will compare the treatment of this scene in two film versions of *Much Ado About Nothing*.
3. Students will evaluate how well each film version of the scene represents the play, both in terms of faithfulness to the original text and in spirit.

Instructional Sequence

While this activity is designed to be completed after students have completed reading Act 1 of *Much Ado About Nothing* by William Shakespeare, it can be completed at any point after that.

1. Pass out the worksheet **Through the Directors' Eyes, located on page 94**.
2. As a class, read aloud the scene from *Much Ado About Nothing* in which Beatrice and Benedick meet in Messina (Act 1, scene 1, lines 93–114 in the *No Fear* edition).
3. Show the sequence from Branagh's film to the class (00:10:00–00:11:19), immediately followed by the same sequence from Whedon's film (00:06:36–00:07:55). Instruct students to only pay attention to the scene and not take any notes.
4. Ask students to take a moment to think about what aspects were different in the two films' versions of the scene. Elicit a few ideas and write them on the board. Tell students they will now re-watch each version specifically to contrast the films. Remind them to pay attention to both literary elements (such as characters and setting) as well as film techniques (such as camera work and framing). Show each scene again, and have students fill in the chart on their worksheet.
5. As a class, have students volunteer their chart answers. For each answer, ask students to explain the impact of the director's choice. For example, ask: *What is the effect of placing Beatrice and Benedick's conversation in public instead of in private?*
6. Have students answer the questions on the worksheet, and then have them share their responses in small groups.
7. As a class, discuss which film version students think is most faithful to Shakespeare and also which they prefer.

CCSS: RL.11-12.7

Differentiated Instruction

This activity can be modified to help all students access learning.

Decrease Difficulty

Provide students with the following aspects to compare in each film scene: coloration, setting, costumes, characters, framing, camera work, and mood.

Increase Difficulty

Have students view and compare other scenes from the movies. The scene in which Margaret disguised as Hero stands in the window is particularly compelling since both film versions show the action instead of simply relating what happened, as Shakespeare does in the play.

PART 3

Worksheets and Handouts

Shakespeare Speak

Overview

Some of the words and phrases Shakespeare uses are so uncommon today that they may sound like another language to the modern reader. This can be discouraging for students as they struggle with Elizabethan vocabulary that inhibits their understanding of a play. Becoming familiar with "Shakespeare speak" will help students to better understand his works and build confidence when studying Shakespeare. Students will use this worksheet to examine and learn common vocabulary used in many of Shakespeare's plays. They will read a term in context, write a definition from that context, and then find a definition from another source.

RL.9-10.4 Determine the meaning of words and phrases as they are used in the text, including figurative and connotative meanings; analyze the cumulative impact of specific word choices on meaning and tone (e.g., how the language evokes a sense of time and place; how it sets a formal or informal tone).

Shakespeare Speak

Some of the words and phrases Shakespeare uses are so uncommon today that they may sound like another language to the modern reader. Yet these terms were commonly used during his day. Becoming familiar with "Shakespeare speak" will help you to better understand his works.

Study the list of words taken from some of Shakespeare's most well-known plays. Read the section of the play in which each word is used. Based on the context, define the word to the best of your ability. Record your definition in the third column. Then, after creating your own definition from the context, provide the dictionary definition in the fourth column. How close was your definition?

Word	Text from the Play	Your Definition Based on Context	Dictionary Definition
beguiled	"Poor ropes, you are beguiled, / Both you and I, for Romeo is exiled." (*No Fear Shakespeare Romeo and Juliet* 3.2.133–134)	tricked or fooled	hoodwinked, deceived (Webster's)
beseech	"I yet beseech your majesty, / If for I want that glib and oily art / To speak and purpose not—since what I well intend[.]" (*No Fear Shakespeare King Lear* 1.1.230–232)		
chide	"Do you not come your tardy son to chide. / That, lapsed in time and passion, lets go by / The important acting of your dread command?" (*No Fear Shakespeare Hamlet* 3.4.108–110)		
entreat	"I do entreat your grace to pardon me. / I know not by what power I am made bold / Nor how it may concern my modesty / In such a presence here to plead my thoughts[.]" (*No Fear Shakespeare A Midsummer Night's Dream* 1.1.58–61)		

Word	Text from the Play	Your Definition Based on Context	Dictionary Definition
canker	"To put down Richard, that sweet lovely rose. / An plant this thorn, this canker, Bolingbroke? / And shall it in more shame be further spoken / That you are fooled, discarded, and shook off / By him for whom these shames you underwent?" (*No Fear Shakespeare Henry IV*, Part 1 1.3.174–178)		
forsworn	"By my knavery (if I had it), then I were. But if you swear by that that is not, you are not forsworn[.]" (*No Fear Shakespeare As You Like It* 1.2.61–63)		
fortune	"Thou know'st that all my fortunes are at sea. / Neither have I money nor commodity / To raise a present sum." (*No Fear Shakespeare The Merchant of Venice* 1.1.179–181)		
haste	"Signior Baptista, my business asketh haste, / And every day I cannot come to woo." (*No Fear Shakespeare The Taming of the Shrew* 2.1.107–108)		
jest	"I knew him, Horatio, a fellow of infinite jest, of most excellent fancy." (*No Fear Shakespeare Hamlet* 5.1.160–161)		
shrift	"Be plain, good son, and homely in thy drift. / Riddling confession finds but riddling shrift." (*No Fear Shakespeare Romeo and Juliet* 2.3.55–56)		

Word	Text from the Play	Your Definition Based on Context	Dictionary Definition
shrive	"I should be glad of his approach. If he have the condition of a saint and the complexion of a devil, I had rather he should shrive me than wive me." (*No Fear Shakespeare The Merchant of Venice* 1.2.112–115)		
sojourn	"The two great princes, France and Burgundy, / Great rivals in our youngest daughter's love. / Long in our court have made their amorous sojourn[.]" (*No Fear Shakespeare King Lear* 1.1.44–46)		
herald	"It is the part of men to fear and tremble / When the most mighty gods by tokens send / Such dreadful heralds to astonish us." (*No Fear Shakespeare Julius Caesar* 1.3.55–57)		
woe	"If e'er thou wast thyself and these woes thine, / Thou and these woes were all for Rosaline." (*No Fear Shakespeare Romeo and Juliet* 2.3.77–78)		
wrought	"How you were borne in hand, how crossed, the instruments, / Who wrought with them, and all things else that might / To half a soul and to a notion crazed / Say, 'Thus did Banquo.'" (*No Fear Shakespeare Macbeth* 3.1.83–86)		

✳sparkteach

Archaic Language

Overview

Although the themes and emotions of Shakespeare's plays remain extraordinarily relevant to the modern student, the archaic language presents challenges to today's learners. This handout sets students up for success with Shakespeare's works by explaining commonly challenging archaic diction in Elizabethan English. Students will study definitions of common pronouns, verbs, and phrases and write modern synonyms to help increase their understanding and retention of what they read.

Archaic Language

Many people struggle with comprehension when reading Shakespeare's plays. One of the reasons for this is that our language has changed enormously since Shakespeare's time. There are many words, phrases, and terms that were in common use then that are no longer used today. There are also words that are still used today but with a different meaning. Words and meanings that have fallen out of common use are referred to as *archaic diction*.

Pronouns

One specific and potentially confusing grammatical element from Shakespeare's time is the use of different words for today's *you* and *your*. Archaic diction is often filled with unfamiliar pronouns, such as *thee* and *thine* and *thou* and *thy*, or familiar pronouns with different meanings, such as the word *you*.

Study the charts to familiarize yourself with common archaic terms.

Archaic Term	Modern Form	Archaic Usage Rule/Grammar
thou	you (singular)	more familiar and informal address, used as the subject of a sentence "Be as well neighbored, pitied, and relieved / As thou my sometime daughter." (*No Fear Shakespeare King Lear* 1.1.120–121)
you	you	more polite and formal address, used as the object of a sentence "And now, Laertes, what's the news with you?" (*No Fear Shakespeare Hamlet* 1.2.42)
thee	you (singular)	referring to a person, used as the object of the sentence "If they do see thee, they will murder thee." (*No Fear Shakespeare Romeo and Juliet* 2.2.70)
you	you (plural)	plural, used when addressing a group "Hence! Home, you idle creatures get you home!" (*No Fear Shakespeare Julius Caesar* 1.1.1)
ye	you (plural)	plural, used to address several people in high positions (formal) also used to address one or more than one person in an informal manner: "If it might please you to enforce no further / The griefs between ye, to forget them quite[.]" (*No Fear Shakespeare Antony and Cleopatra* 2.2.107–108)
ye	the	definite article; to modify a noun in the same way *the* is used today "Ye Roman gods!" (*No Fear Shakespeare Coriolanus* 1.6.7)

Archaic Term	Modern Form	Archaic Usage Rule/Grammar
thy	your	singular—followed by a word that begins with a consonant sound "So well thy words become thee as thy wounds[.]" (*No Fear Shakespeare Macbeth* 1.2.43)
thine	your	indicates ownership or possession; usually singular followed by a word that begins with a vowel sound "By giving liberty unto thine eyes;" (*No Fear Shakespeare Romeo and Juliet* 1.1.217)

Common Verbs

Archaic Term	Modern Form
'tis	it is
'twas	it was
'twere	it were
'twix	between two things; betwixt
art	are
doth	do
durst	dared
hast	have
hath	have
wilt	will

Note: Verbs ending in -est are related to the second-person pronoun *thou*.

Review the following chart. Fill in the fourth column with modern synonyms, idioms, or colloquial expressions for each archaic word or phrase provided.

Greetings, Common Words, and Expressions

Archaic Word or Phrase	Modern Form	Informal Definition	Modern Synonyms
adieu	goodbye	bye	
alack/alas	expression of sorrow often an exclamation	oh, no	
anon	in a little while, at once	in a second	
ay (aye)	yes—affirmative response	yes	
doff	to take off or remove or rid oneself of	take off	
ere	before	before	
fie	an exclamation to express disgust	Seriously?	
God ye good morrow; God ye good den (good den); God ye good e'en	good morning good day good evening	hello	
hie	to go quickly	hurry up	

Archaic Word or Phrase	Modern Form	Informal Definition	Modern Synonyms
hither	to this place, here	here	
thither	to that place, there	there	
how now	How are you?	hello	
naught	nothing	all for nothing	
nay	no—negative response	no	
sirrah	used to address a servant or a person of lower stature	N/A	
whence	from where	from where	
wherefore	why	why	
withal	together	together	
yea	yes—affirmative response	yes	
yonder	in the distance	over there	

Shakespearean Stage Directions

Overview

Shakespeare often directed and acted in his plays. He wrote with an actor's sensibility and with an understanding that he would be there to guide the drama. Therefore, Shakespeare offers very little in the way of stage directions compared to modern playwrights. However, there are some consistent stage directions that Shakespeare did use, which this handout explains. Understanding these directions will help students better visualize the action of the play as they read.

Shakespearean Stage Directions

Shakespeare often directed and acted in his plays. He wrote with an actor's sensibility and with an understanding that he would be there to guide the drama. Therefore, Shakespeare offers very little in the way of stage directions compared to modern playwrights and even some of his contemporaries. In fact, Shakespeare embeds most of the characters' actions within the language of the play, leaving it up to the reader and director to decipher a character's motivation, attitude, or actions based on the inferences provided in the dialogue itself. However, there are some common stage directions Shakespeare does include that should be understood by the modern reader. The following is a list of commonly occurring stage directions in Shakespeare's plays.

Coming and Going

The most common stage directions in any play are used to indicate the coming and going of characters. Shakespeare uses simple directions to indicate such action.

Enter: indicates the entrance of a character or characters onto the stage

Exit: indicates a character exiting the stage

Exeunt: indicates the exit of multiple characters from the stage (Exeunt is Latin, the archaic third-person plural form of "exit." The term's literal translation is "they leave.")

Re-enter: indicates that a character that has recently exited the stage has returned to it

Important Moments

The entrance of an important character, such as a prince or king, and important moments like a battle are often announced with a particular flair or fanfare. The following indicators are used to highlight important characters or events.

Alarum: an archaic form of alarm used to indicate a battle is about to occur

Flourish: indicates the playing of drums and trumpets, which is used to indicate the entrance of a king

Sennet: similar to a flourish, a trumpet call signaling a group of people proceeding across the stage

Hautboys / Cornet / Trumpet: indicates that wind instruments are played to highlight or announce an important character's entrance or some other fanfare

Drum: indicates the playing of a drum

Staging

Staging, an essential element in any production, is the manner in which a play is presented on stage. Some critics believe that some of the more precise stage directions were added to Shakespeare's plays when published after his death. However, regardless of their origin, the plays offer some direction regarding movement and direction of characters or action on and around the stage. Since most of Shakespeare's plays were staged in his Globe Theatre, some of the stage directions in his plays refer specifically to the unique setup of this space.

Above / Balcony: indicates the action or direction takes place above the stage; this would indicate the use of an upper level such as one of the balconies above the stage in the Globe Theatre. The musicians would often perform from the balcony area.

Advances: the character moves forward or up to another character; sometimes indicates an aggressive action

Aside: suggests that the character speaks his or her thoughts and inner feelings directly to the audience without revealing them to the other characters on the stage; this narrative technique allows for a deeper understanding of a character's motivations and actions and is often used to create dramatic irony, revealing details to the audience that the characters on the stage are unaware of

Arras: refers to the curtain or tapestry on the stage, such as the one Polonius hides behind when he is killed by Hamlet

Below: Shakespeare's Globe Theatre was known to have a trapdoor embedded in the stage. While actors would refer to this door as "hell," stage directions refer to this area as "below." The action might also take place off the stage, where the audience traditionally stands.

Excursion: indicates a battle or fight occurring on the stage; this usually is shown by a group of people fighting across the stage or in the scene's background

Severally: the archaic equivalent of separately; indicates that actors enter from several different areas of the stage

Torches: suggests that the characters entering the stage are carrying lit torches

Within: indicates that the character speaking or being spoken to is offstage; in the context of the story, the character may be in another room or area calling to the character on the stage

More Complex Action

Shakespeare is often vague when it comes to complicated interactions. For example, in *Romeo and Juliet* the fight scenes between Tybalt and Mercutio, as well as between Romeo and Tybalt—scenes meant to convey the highest point of action in the play—are described with two simple words: "They fight."

Alternatively, Shakespeare's plays, at times, offer some rather clear direction, such as when, in *The Winter's Tale*, stage directions indicate that Antigonus "Exit[s], pursued by bear."

Basic Structural Elements

When reading Shakespeare, it is also important to understand some basic structural elements in his plays. These elements divide up the plot, pace the action, provide opportunities for settings to be changed, and make it easier for the audience to follow along.

Act: Shakespeare's plays are always divided into five acts. This structure was influenced by the Roman playwright Seneca and Aristotle's *Poetics* and forms the basic structure of Shakespeare's plays. The five-act pattern creates a basic story arc, where act one presents the exposition, act two develops the conflict, act three usually imparts the highest point of action or brings the conflict to a climactic moment, act four begins the falling action, and act five delivers the resolution.

Scene: Each act in Shakespeare's plays is divided into scenes. These divisions are often based on the place and time of the action in the scene. Most scenes will take place in one location and focus on a single set of characters.

Dramatis personae: a list of characters that appears at the beginning of the play's manuscript

Prologue: an introduction to the play recited by a single actor referred to as the chorus; the purpose of the chorus and prologue is to fill in expository, or background, information.

Epilogue: a short commentary regarding the meaning of the play spoken at the end, usually by a character reflecting on the play's events

Film Terms

Overview

Film can be an effective means of helping your students engage with literature, particularly more traditionally difficult texts, such as Shakespearean plays. Film is also an important medium for visual learners, who often appreciate seeing literature come to life on screen. This handout gives definitions for common film terms so that students can more effectively discuss the art of filmmaking and compare and contrast films with written texts to deepen their understanding and analysis of literary works.

Film Terms

Term	Definition/ Explanation
background	events and images in the rear of the stage or back of the scene
blocking	figuring out or planning where actors move or stand on the stage or set
	setting the camera in a particular place to capture character placement, lighting arrangement, and movement
building a scene or building suspense in a scene	using a device, such as intensifying music, to increase a scene's pace or suspense and bring it toward a climactic moment
camera angle	the point of view or perspective of the camera from which the scene is shot
	Camera angles are described using the direction from which the shot is taken relative to the action, such as *low, high, neutral,* and *long shot.* Some specific shot terms include the following:
	aerial shot: a shot filmed from high above using a crane, plane, or drone
	boom shot: a shot taken from a high angle and sometimes involving movement of the camera
	close-up shot: a shot for which the camera is zoomed in, showing the subject's head or an object at close range
	dolly shot: a shot using a steadying device, such as a dolly or truck, to move the camera toward or away from the action
	long shot: a shot taken from far away, designed to make a person seem small compared to the background
	medium shot: a shot showing a person from the waist up
	pan: to move the camera either left or right across an area
	Note: *Panning* only refers to long horizontal movements in one direction.
	point of view shot: a shot that shows the world through a character's perspective
	tilt: the vertical version of panning—to move the camera either up or down
	tracking shot: a shot following a subject while the subject is in motion
	zoom: a stationary shot that zooms in or out from a subject, creating the feeling that the camera is moving
cast	the actors and performers that appear in the film
choreographer	the person responsible for coming up with and directing organized sequences of action and movement in the film or on a stage
choreography	the directing of organized sequences of action and movement, such as fighting or dancing, in a film or on the stage

Term	Definition/ Explanation
cinematography	the art of capturing images or sequences on film, specifically in reference to the use of lighting, camera angles, imagery, lenses, and blocking to artistically capture a scene
coda	a final image that functions as an epilogue for the film
composition	the organization or arrangement of shapes, lines, color, movement, and lighting the way a scene is visually constructed for effect
contrast	stark differences usually created by light and shadow
costuming / wardrobe	the costumes actors wear in a film Note: The style and period of clothing and accessories can create verisimilitude (the presence of reality in fiction) and helps to establish mood and atmosphere.
cut / editing and transitions	a sudden change in camera angle, location, scene (i.e., cutting from one scene to another) the director or film editor literally cutting film and splicing it together in certain ways to create a clear and effective action sequence Note: There are many types of cuts. The type of cut refers to the way in which the director splices scenes together. Some examples: **cross-cutting:** usually used to create action by cutting between two events in the same location. The scene's focus moves back and forth between two or more characters to build suspense. **dissolve:** when one image gradually fades out while transitioning to another **fade in / out:** the image slowly fades into the scene or fades out to, usually, a black screen **jump cut:** a quick jump between two similar but different camera angles focused on the same subject in order to give the effect of the subject or time jumping forward **montage:** a series of shots edited together to show the passage of time **wipe:** one image or scene is pushed off the side of the screen by another
director	the person who guides the action and creation of the film at all levels of production, who is responsible for telling the story, and who is credited for the film as an author would be credited for writing a book There are often many directors on a film set who specialize in certain areas of production, such as the director of photography, the music director, etc.
editing	the post-filming process of arranging, cutting, and structuring the film to create a complete and cohesive story
fade	when an image or music fades in or out of a scene, or when a scene fades from darkness to light or sound to silence
filter	device used to change the lighting in a film to create a specific effect or atmosphere
focus	the sharpness or distortion of an image created by the manipulation of a camera lens

*spark*teach   **49**

Term	Definition/ Explanation
foreground	where a scene's main action occurs
fourth wall	a term that refers to the audience Note: The term is often used when characters "break" the fourth wall and talk directly to the audience.
frame	what is captured by the camera in a single image
genre	the style or type of film, based on thematic or plot elements Some genre examples are musicals, westerns, horror, romantic comedy, and action adventure.
juxtaposition	the positioning of two images, characters, objects, or scenes together for the purpose of comparison Juxtaposition establishes stark contrast or relationships between two characters or scenes.
lighting	the manipulation of light and darkness used by the cinematographer to create mood and atmosphere Some specific types of lighting include the following: *backlighting*: the subject is lit from behind, creating a shadow or silhouette for the camera *fill light*: a light is placed to the side of an actor or scene in order to eliminate shadows in the background of the scene *key light*: the central or main lighting for a scene *mood lighting*: lighting used to create a particular mood or atmosphere; usually involves colored lights and shadows
location	the place where the scene is filmed
makeup	the use of cosmetics, costuming, masks, and other elements to enhance or distort human features Makeup artists are responsible for everything from simple beauty makeup to the design and development of creatures and monsters.
mise en scène	backdrop, sets, props, actors, and lighting This French term literally translates to "placing on stage."
motif	a recurring image or idea in a film
props	an object used in a scene (shortened from "theatrical property")
scene	many shots taken in a single location that focus on a single action
script	the text containing the dialogue and story for the film
set	the stage or stages in which the actions for the film are recorded

Term	Definition/ Explanation
soundtrack	the music written for or played during various film sequences Music enhances mood and atmosphere.
special effects	illusions and visual tricks used to create impossible images, objects, or events Note: Most special effects today are created by CGI (computer generated images), but there are still many mechanical and nondigital optical illusions used to create special effects.
tone	the way a film "feels" or how a film is supposed to make the audience feel Tone is set through the mood and atmosphere of the film. The tone of a film can be humorous, serious, shocking, satiric, sad, etc.

Metaphor and Simile

Overview

Metaphor and simile are two of the most commonly taught, studied, and tested literary devices. Understanding these prolific devices will enable students to more fully understand and appreciate great works of literature. Students will use this worksheet to learn about metaphors and similes and the distinctions between them. They will then dissect examples of each from notable works of literature.

RL.9-10.4 Determine the meaning of words and phrases as they are used in the text, including figurative and connotative meanings; analyze the cumulative impact of specific word choices on meaning and tone (e.g., how the language evokes a sense of time and place; how it sets a formal or informal tone).

Metaphor and Simile

Abstractions by definition are difficult to understand. Since the purpose of literature in all of its forms is, ultimately, to convey some abstract concept about the human condition in a meaningful manner, writers often employ literary and poetic devices that make the abstract qualities of life's experiences concrete and relatable to a reader. Abstract concepts like *love*, *jealousy*, *fear*, and *hate* have many complex and nuanced characteristics. In order to clearly convey these concepts, writers often rely on comparisons in the form of figurative language. Two of the most commonly used forms of figurative language are metaphor and simile.

1. Understand the terms.

   A *metaphor* **is a direct comparison of two unlike things. A metaphor is presented through words or phrases that are not literally true.**

   A *simile* **functions the same way as a metaphor, but the comparison is made through the use of words such as** *like*, *as*, *than*, **and** *so*.

2. Practice making abstract connections: Choose an abstract idea from the following list and create similes by relating the idea to something concrete, yet seemingly unrelated to the abstraction. Then explain why the two elements are similar.

Abstractions: *love, hate, jealousy, anger, fear, excitement, hardship, peace, family, prejudice*
Use the following template to develop the simile:

(Abstract idea) is like **(concrete element)** because **(explanation)**.

For example: **Love** is like **a bacon cheeseburger** because **it is fulfilling and delicious but can sometimes lead to unforeseen problems.**

_____ is like _____ because _____ .

_____ is like _____ because _____ .

_____ is like _____ because _____ .

_____ is like _____ because _____ .

*spark*teach   **53**

3. Explain the comparison created by the following metaphors and similes. First, explain the abstract idea and the concrete element it is being compared to. Then explain the concept conveyed by the comparison.

What happens **to a dream deferred**?

Does it dry up

Like **a raisin in the sun**?

(from "Harlem" by Langston Hughes)

Abstract Idea	Concrete Element	Relationship: (abstract idea) **is like** (concrete element) **because . . .**
a dream deferred	a raisin in the sun	A dream deferred is like a raisin in the sun because

All the **world's a stage**, And all the **men and women** merely **players**[.]

(from *As You Like It* by William Shakespeare)

Abstract Idea	Concrete Element	Relationship: (abstract idea) **is like** (concrete element) **because . . .**
world	stage	A world is like a stage because
men and women	players	

The **bank**—the **monster** has to have profits all the time. It can't wait. It'll die.

(from *The Grapes of Wrath* by John Steinbeck)

Abstract Idea	Concrete Element	Relationship: (abstract idea) **is like** (concrete element) **because . . .**
bank	monster	

4. Now it's your turn! Identify the abstract and concrete comparable elements in the examples, and then explain how the abstract idea and concrete element are alike.

I wandered lonely as a cloud

That floats on high o'er vales and hills[.]

(from "I Wandered Lonely as a Cloud" by William Wordsworth)

Abstract Idea	Concrete Element	Relationship: (abstract idea) is like (concrete element) because . . .

Let us go then, you and I,

When the evening is spread out against the sky

Like a patient etherized upon a table[.]

(from "The Love Song of J. Alfred Prufrock" by T.S. Eliot)

Abstract Idea	Concrete Element	Relationship: (abstract idea) is like (concrete element) because . . .

5. For one final challenge, try to identify the abstract and concrete ideas in this extended passage and explain the relationships created through the metaphoric comparison.

And that night there came on a terrific storm, with driving rain, awful claps of thunder and blinding sheets of lightning. He covered his head with the bed-clothes and waited in a horror of suspense for his doom; for he had not the shadow of a doubt that all this hubbub was about him. He believed he had taxed the forbearance of the powers above to the extremity of endurance and that this was the result. It might have seemed to him a waste of pomp and ammunition to kill a bug with a battery of artillery, but there seemed nothing incongruous about the getting up such an expensive thunderstorm as this to knock the turf from under an insect like himself.

(from *The Adventures of Tom Sawyer* by Mark Twain)

Abstract Idea	Concrete Element	Relationship: (abstract idea) is like (concrete element) because . . .

Abstract Idea	Concrete Element	Relationship: (abstract idea) is like (concrete element) because . . .

Renaissance Concepts of Love and Marriage

Overview

Much Ado About Nothing draws much of its plot, humor, and drama from the rituals and social mores surrounding courtship, love, and marriage. This handout provides relevant background information about basic concepts that were crucial to the development of matrimonial relationships during the Renaissance. Use this handout to ensure that students understand how marriage rituals both were different in Renaissance times and were reflected in Shakespeare's work. Discuss the content as a class, and allow students to offer personal opinions and make cross-curricular connections.

Renaissance Concepts of Love and Marriage

Courtship

Only entering the English language toward the end of the sixteenth century, the word *courtship* describes the period in which a couple engages in social activities in order to get to know each other better with hopes of getting married. During Shakespeare's time, friends and family played a primary role in courtship, often serving as matchmakers, much as Beatrice and Benedick's friends did. While young people could meet on their own—they were at liberty to meet and mix in public places, like markets and dances—if a man was interested in a woman, he asked her father for permission to court. This request showed that his intentions were serious. A courting couple could attend social events together and often exchanged gifts that had symbolic meaning.

Betrothal and Marriage

Once a couple completed the courtship rituals, they entered into a betrothal period by becoming formally engaged to be married. A betrothal was a legally binding relationship that could last as long as a year. Couples publicly pledged themselves to one another in a ceremony in front of a priest. (In England, this tradition was called *handfasting*.) If the man or woman wanted to break the betrothal, church lawyers had to get involved. The Council of Trent, which met from 1545 to 1563, however, brought reforms to the process of betrothal and marriage for members of the Catholic Church, which comprised most Europeans. To be lawfully married, the couple had to receive the Church's consent, by either purchasing a license or reading the "banns," which announced the names of the couple and their intention to marry. Either process took a month to finalize. Drawing on long tradition, the couple exchanged rings to signify that they were no longer betrothed but now married.

Arranged Marriages

In the Renaissance, marriage was not seen as a matter of love between two people but rather as a practical matter. Marriage involved not just individuals but families, fortunes, and communities as well. Sometimes families sought an economic alliance, such as the joining of property. Other times they wanted to forge or strengthen political alliances or even unite kingdoms. Upper-class

*sparkteach   61

families arranged their children's marriages, often with little thought to the wishes of their children or whether the couple even liked one another. Brides in the Italian Renaissance tended to be significantly younger than their spouses; the legal age for marriage was fourteen, and these girls could be married to men twice their age. As part of the marriage arrangements, a dowry—which was money, goods, or property that the bride brought to her husband when they married —was agreed upon. Among the peasant class, parents arranged their children's marriages far less frequently. Members of the lower classes had more freedom to meet potential partners and embark on courtship routines in their daily lives.

Married Life

Married men and women had specific roles and responsibilities in their relationships. Men held complete authority over their wives. Married women had little or no decision-making authority nor could they generally own property. While peasant women labored in the fields and middle-class women might help tend their husbands' businesses, women were always expected to take care of the home and children. Men, on the other hand, had the obligation to support and protect their wives. Married men and women were viewed as providing companionship to one another, not romantic love. Even if a man and a woman no longer served as good companions to one another, divorce was forbidden. While marriages were occasionally annulled, most marriages ended when one partner died. Since many people died young during the Renaissance, many adults married two or even three times.

Representations of Love in Literature

The concept of love in Renaissance poetry manifested itself in different ways. In the 1300s, Italian poets Dante Alighieri and Petrarch, working from the concept of courtly love with its roots in the love stories of knights and ladies, developed a poetry that idealized love itself. These authors created a perfect female who served as the source of inspiration for her beloved. This ideal of love transcended daily life and did not truly reflect the relationships of mortal men and women. Later poets focused on Platonic, or non-romantic, ties; instead of existing as a fleshy, earthy concept, love became a path to a higher virtue and led to a better understanding of the divine. Pastoral poetry was also popular during the Renaissance. Again drawing from earlier traditions, pastoral poems glorified the simple life of shepherds and nymphs who lived in the countryside, far from the corruption of the urban world.

*sparkteach **63**

Deciphering Dogberry's Malapropisms

Overview

In Dogberry from *Much Ado About Nothing*, William Shakespeare creates an amazing buffoon of a character who consistently misuses difficult words to comic effect. Students will use this worksheet to understand malapropisms, examine sentences that include them, define the incorrectly used word, and then replace it with the correct word. Consider extending practice of malapropisms by having students work in groups to write a few of their own.

Answer Key

Sentence with Malapropism	Real Definition of Malapropism	Word Dogberry Should Have Used
"Nay, that were a punishment too good for them, if they should have any **allegiance** in them, being chosen for the Prince's watch." (*No Fear*: 3.3.4–6)	*loyalty*	*disloyalty*
"You are thought here to be the most **senseless** and fit man for the constable of the watch; therefore bear you the lantern." (*No Fear*: 3.3.19–21)	*dumb*	*sensible*
"You shall also make no noise in the streets; for, for the watch to babble and to talk is most **tolerable** and not to be endured." (*No Fear*: 3.3.31–33)	*bearable*	*intolerable*
"Marry, sir, I would have some confidence with you that **decerns** [discerns] you nearly." (*No Fear*: 3.5.2–3)	*detects*	*concerns*
"Comparisons are **odorous**. (*No Fear*: 3.5.14)	*smelly*	*odious*

Sentence with Malapropism	Real Definition of Malapropism	Word Dogberry Should Have Used
"Yea, an 'twere a thousand pound more than 'tis, for I hear as good **exclamation** on your Worship as of any man in the city, and though I be but a poor man, I am glad to hear it." (*No Fear*: 3.5.21–23)	*sudden cry*	*acclamation*
"Our watch, sir, have indeed **comprehended** two **aspicious** [auspicious] persons, and we would have them this morning examined before your worship." (*No Fear*: 3.5.39–41)	*understood* *promising*	*apprehended* *suspicious*
"Only get the learned writer to set down our **excommunication** and meet me at the jail." (*No Fear*: 3.5.54–55)	*exclusion from a Christian church*	*meeting (for examination)*
"Why, this is flat **perjury**, to call a prince's brother villain." (*No Fear*: 4.2.35–36)	*lying under oath*	*treachery*
"Thou wilt be condemned into everlasting **redemption** for this." (*No Fear*: 4.2.49–50)	*atonement for sin*	*damnation*
"Dost thou not **suspect** my place? Dost thou not **suspect** my years?" (*No Fear*: 4.2.66–67)	*believe someone is guilty*	*respect*

RL.11-12.3 Analyze the impact of the author's choices regarding how to develop and relate elements of a story or drama (e.g., where a story is set, how the action is ordered, how the characters are introduced and developed).

RL.11-12.4 Determine the meaning of words and phrases as they are used in the text, including figurative and connotative meanings; analyze the impact of specific word choices on meaning and tone, including words with multiple meanings or language that is particularly fresh, engaging, or beautiful. (Include Shakespeare as well as other authors.)

L.11-12.4 Determine or clarify the meaning of unknown and multiple-meaning words and phrases based on grades 11–12 reading and content, choosing flexibly from a range of strategies.

L.11-12.5 Determine or clarify the meaning of unknown and multiple-meaning words and phrases based on grades 11–12 reading and content, choosing flexibly from a range of strategies.

Deciphering Dogberry's Malapropisms

A *malapropism* is the misuse or distortion of a word in a way that is unintentionally humorous, particularly when the word sounds similar to the real word but is ludicrous in context. In fact, the word *malapropism* derives from the French term *mal à propos*, which means "inappropriate."

The constable Dogberry exemplifies the art of malapropism in Shakespeare's *Much Ado About Nothing*. In an effort to sound smart, Dogberry uses numerous "big" words, but incorrectly. These mistakes lead to much humor as they demonstrate Dogberry's much-inflated ego, but they also lead to declarations that make no sense and reflect the exact opposite of the intended statement.

In column 1: Read the sentences from the play that contain malapropisms.

In column 2: Write the correct meaning of the bolded word. (Remember it has been used inappropriately by Dogberry.)

In column 3: Record the word that *should* have been used.

Note: You may consult the text and a dictionary or thesaurus, if necessary.

Sentence with Malapropism	Real Definition of Malapropism	Word Dogberry Should Have Used
"Nay, that were a punishment too good for them, if they should have any **allegiance** in them, being chosen for the Prince's watch." (*No Fear*: 3.3.4–6)	*loyalty*	*disloyalty*
"You are thought here to be the most **senseless** and fit man for the constable of the watch; therefore bear you the lantern." (*No Fear*: 3.3.19–21)		
"You shall also make no noise in the streets; for, for the watch to babble and to talk is most **tolerable** and not to be endured." (*No Fear*: 3.3.31–33)		

Sentence with Malapropism	Real Definition of Malapropism	Word Dogberry Should Have Used
"Marry, sir, I would have some confidence with you that **decerns** [discerns] you nearly." (*No Fear*: 3.5.2–3)		
"Comparisons are **odorous**." (*No Fear*: 3.5.14)		
"Yea, an 'twere a thousand pound more than 'tis, for I hear as good **exclamation** on your Worship as of any man in the city, and though I be but a poor man, I am glad to hear it." (*No Fear*: 3.5.21–23)		
"Our watch, sir, have indeed **comprehended** two **aspicious** [auspicious] persons, and we would have them this morning examined before your worship." (*No Fear*: 3.5.39–41)		
"Only get the learned writer to set down our **excommunication** and meet me at the jail." (*No Fear*: 3.5.54–55)		
"Why, this is flat **perjury**, to call a prince's brother villain." (*No Fear*: 4.2.35–36)		
"Thou wilt be condemned into everlasting **redemption** for this." (*No Fear*: 4.2.49–50)		
"Dost thou not **suspect** my place? Dost thou not **suspect** my years?" (*No Fear*: 4.2.66–67)		

*spark*teach

Beatrice in Her Own Words

Overview

Beatrice is one of Shakespeare's most famous female characters, and her sparring matches with Benedick create some of his most lively dialogue. Beatrice reveals much of her character and personality through her words. Students will use this worksheet to summarize passages that provide a better understanding of Beatrice and make notes on what her words reveal about her character. Then students will discuss Beatrice's modernity in small groups. Pass out this worksheet after students have finished reading the play.

RL.11-12.1 Cite strong and thorough textual evidence to support analysis of what the text says explicitly as well as inferences drawn from the text, including determining where the text leaves matters uncertain.

RL.11-12.2 Determine two or more themes or central ideas of a text and analyze their development over the course of the text, including how they interact and build on one another to produce a complex account; provide an objective summary of the text.

SL.11-12.1 Initiate and participate effectively in a range of collaborative discussions (one-on-one, in groups, and teacher-led) with diverse partners on grades 11–12 topics, texts, and issues, building on others' ideas and expressing their own clearly and persuasively.

Beatrice in Her Own Words

Beatrice is a woman of many words, both witty and serious, in *Much Ado About Nothing*. What do her own words reveal about her personality? Use this worksheet to find out.

In column 1: Read Beatrice's speeches.

In column 2: Summarize each quote.

In column 3: Evaluate what her words reveal about her character.

Finally, discuss in what ways Beatrice is a woman typical of her time and in what ways she represents a more modern woman.

Passage	Summary	What Words Reveal About Beatrice
"Alas, he gets nothing by that. In our last conflict four of his five wits went halting off, and now is the whole man governed with one, so that if he have wit enough to keep himself warm, let him bear it for a difference between himself and his horse, for it is all the wealth that he hath left to be known a reasonable creature. Who is his companion now? He hath every month a new sworn brother." (*No Fear*: 1.1.52–58)	*Beatrice bested Benedick in their last verbal skirmish so severely that he only had one of his five wits left, making him hardly smarter than his horse. Who is his friend right now? Every month he has a new best friend.*	*Beatrice thinks she is smarter than Benedick and comes out on top in their verbal sparring. She also knows that he flits from one friend to the next.*
"What should I do with him? Dress him in my apparel and make him my waiting gentlewoman? He that hath a beard is more than a youth, and he that hath no beard is less than a man; and he that is more than a youth is not for me, and he that is less than a man, I am not for him." (*No Fear*: 2.1.28–32)		

*spark*teach

Passage	Summary	What Words Reveal About Beatrice
"Not till God make men of some other metal than earth. Would it not grieve a woman to be overmastered with a piece of valiant dust? To make an account of her life to a clod of wayward marl? No, uncle, I'll none. Adam's sons are my brethren, and truly I hold it a sin to match in my kindred." (*No Fear*: 2.1.49–53)		
"The fault will be in the music, cousin, if you be not wooed in good time. If the Prince be too important, tell him there is measure in everything, and so dance out the answer. For hear me, Hero, wooing, wedding, and repenting is as a Scotch jig, a measure, and a cinquepace. The first suit is hot and hasty like a Scotch jig, and full as fantastical; the wedding, mannerly modest as a measure, full of state and ancientry; and then comes repentance, and with his bad legs falls into the cinquepace faster and faster till he sink into his grave." (*No Fear*: 2.1.56–65)		

Passage	Summary	What Words Reveal About Beatrice
"What fire is in mine ears? Can this be true? Stand I condemned for pride and scorn so much? Contempt, farewell, and maiden pride, adieu! No glory lives behind the back of such. And Benedick, love on; I will requite thee, Taming my wild heart to thy loving hand. If thou dost love, my kindness shall incite thee To bind our loves up in a holy band. For others say thou dost deserve, and I Believe it better than reportingly." (*No Fear*: 3.1.113–122)		
"Is he not approved in the height a villain, that hath slandered, scorned, dishonored my kinswoman? Oh, that I were a man! What, bear her in hand until they come to take hands and then, with public accusation, uncovered slander, unmitigated rancor—O God, that I were a man! I would eat his heart in the marketplace." (*No Fear*: 4.1.297–302)		
"Princes and counties! Surely, a princely testimony, a goodly count, Count Comfect, a sweet gallant, surely! Oh, that I were a man for his sake! Or that I had any friend would be a man for my sake! But manhood is melted into curtsies, valor into compliment, and men are only turned into tongue, and trim ones too. He is now as valiant as Hercules that only tells a lie and swears it. I cannot be a man with wishing, therefore I will die a woman with grieving." (*No Fear*: 4.1.309–316)		

Passage	Summary	What Words Reveal About Beatrice
"In spite of your heart, I think. Alas, poor heart, if you spite it for my sake, I will spite it for yours, for I will never love that which my friend hates." (*No Fear*: 5.2.53–54)		
"I would not deny you, but, by this good day, I yield upon great persuasion, and partly to save your life, for I was told you were in a consumption." (*No Fear*: 5.4.97–99)		

Love and Marriage

Overview

Love and marriage emerge as important themes in *Much Ado About Nothing*. Students will use this worksheet to explore and better understand how these two themes develop and intersect in the play. They will review selected passages about love and marriage and add passages of their own. Then they will consider how ideas about love and marriage in the play reflect (or don't) those that we have today. You can have students work individually or in small groups, and they can respond to the final prompt orally or in writing.

Answer Key

Sample Student Response

Sample response for the final prompt:

The characters all express negative thoughts around love. After thinking he got tricked by Don Pedro, Claudio vows to never trust anyone, even friends, when it comes to managing his love affairs. Benedick displays cynicism by proclaiming that he only will love a woman who meets so many standards that it is clear he never expects to find her. Beatrice turns love into a violent emotion, demanding that Benedick prove his love to her by killing Claudio.

Marriage is seen as having little to do with love. As Hero's father, Leonato has the right to expect Hero to marry who he wants; thus marriage is about what the parent deems important. Hero, who hardly knows Claudio, seems unhappy on her wedding day, which reinforces her father's statement. Don Pedro, who arranged the marriage, sees the relationship only in how it reflects back on him; now it reflects poorly since Hero has been publicly declared to be unvirtuous.

In some ways, ideas about love and marriage in the Renaissance were similar to ideas today. People were picky about who they thought was good enough for them, and some people just wanted to play the field and not settle down. Others thought if someone was in love with you, it gave you power over them. However, Renaissance ideas were very different when it came to how women were treated. In Shakespeare's time, women had little say in who they married and just had to obey their father's wishes. Women also were not supposed to have sexual feelings and could be dishonored if they had any sexual contacts before marriage.

RL.11-12.1 Cite strong and thorough textual evidence to support analysis of what the text says explicitly as well as inferences drawn from the text, including determining where the text leaves matters uncertain.

RL.11-12.2 Determine two or more themes or central ideas of a text and analyze their development over the course of the text, including how they interact and build on one another to produce a complex account; provide an objective summary of the text.

W.11–12.2 Write informative/explanatory texts, including the narration of historical events, scientific procedures/experiments, or technical processes.

Love and Marriage

Love and marriage monopolize much of the characters' thoughts in Shakespeare's *Much Ado About Nothing* and emerge as interconnected but not interchangeable themes. Read the following passages that express ideas about love, and then add two more passages about love from the play.

Claudio
'Tis certain so, the Prince woos for himself.
Friendship is constant in all other things
Save in the office and affairs of love.
Therefore all hearts in love use their own tongues.
Let every eye negotiate for itself
And trust no agent, for beauty is a witch
Against whose charms faith melteth into blood.

(*No Fear*: 2.1.145–151)

Beatrice
I love you with so much of my heart that none is left to protest.

Benedick
Come, bid me do anything for thee.

Beatrice
Kill Claudio.

Benedick
Ha! Not for wide world.

Beatrice
You kill me to deny it. Farewell. . . .

Benedick
Tarry, good Beatrice. By this hand, I love thee.

Beatrice
Use it for my love some other way than swearing by it.

(*No Fear*: 4.1.283–318)

Ideas About Love

Benedick
I will not be sworn but love may transform me to an oyster, [/] but I'll take my oath on it, till he have made an oyster of me, [/] he shall never make me such a fool. One woman is fair, yet [/] I am well; another is wise, yet I am well; another virtuous, [/] yet I am well; but till all graces be in one woman, one [/] woman shall not come in my grace. Rich she shall be, that's [/] certain; wise, or I'll none; virtuous, or I'll never cheapen [/] her; fair, or I'll never look on her; mild, or come not near [/] me; noble, or not I for an angel; of good discourse, an [/] excellent musician, and her hair shall be of what color it [/] please God. Ha!

(*No Fear*: 2.3.21–31)

Now repeat that process and complete the graphic organizer "Ideas About Marriage." Add two more passages from the play that deal with marriage.

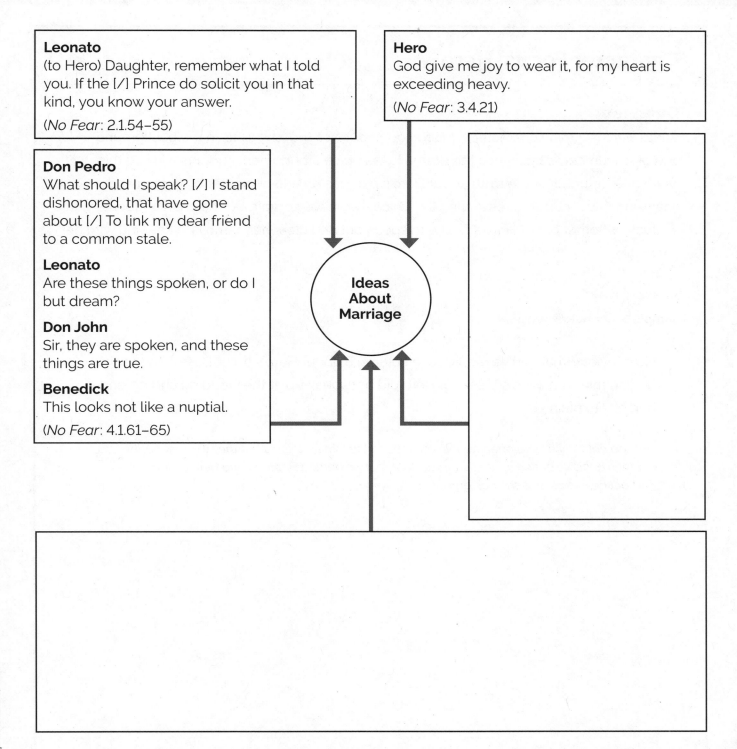

Leonato
(to Hero) Daughter, remember what I told you. If the [/] Prince do solicit you in that kind, you know your answer.

(*No Fear*: 2.1.54–55)

Don Pedro
What should I speak? [/] I stand dishonored, that have gone about [/] To link my dear friend to a common stale.

Leonato
Are these things spoken, or do I but dream?

Don John
Sir, they are spoken, and these things are true.

Benedick
This looks not like a nuptial.

(*No Fear*: 4.1.61–65)

Hero
God give me joy to wear it, for my heart is exceeding heavy.

(*No Fear*: 3.4.21)

Ideas About Marriage

Finally, review your quotes in both graphic organizers to consider how different characters perceive the concepts of love and marriage, and determine if they are similar to ideas about love and marriage today.

*sparkteach **75**

Character Focus: Hero

Overview

While Hero is a main character in *Much Ado About Nothing*, she lurks in the background and often remains silent while the drama takes place around her. Students will use this worksheet to uncover the truth about Hero's personality and character by finding and analyzing relevant passages in the play. Once they have completed the chart, students will evaluate whether or not Hero's failure to speak out and clear her name is in keeping with her character.

Answer Key

Sample Student Response

Now review what you've recorded in column 3 about Hero's traits. Based on this list, do you think it makes sense that Hero did not speak up at the wedding and defend herself? Explain.

No, I do not. While Hero often remains silent and lets others think what they want about her, she did take decisive action in another important matter: getting Beatrice and Benedick together. This action shows that she has gumption.

RL.11-12.1 Cite strong and thorough textual evidence to support analysis of what the text says explicitly as well as inferences drawn from the text, including determining where the text leaves matters uncertain.

RL.11-12.6 Analyze a case in which grasping a point of view requires distinguishing what is directly stated in a text from what is really meant (e.g., satire, sarcasm, irony, or understatement).

W.11-12.3 Write narratives to develop real or imagined experiences or events using effective technique, well-chosen details, and well-structured event sequences.

Character Focus: Hero

Much of the drama in Shakespeare's *Much Ado About Nothing* revolves around the relationship between Hero and Claudio. However, Hero has remarkably little to say. So what is Hero really like? As you read Acts 1 through 3, use this chart to make notes about Hero's personality, paying attention to both how she reveals her personality through her own words and actions and how others perceive her. Then, use your completed chart to answer the question below the chart.

Text About Hero	What Text Says	What Text Reveals About Hero
Hero Now, Ursula, when Beatrice doth come, As we do trace this alley up and down, Our talk must only be of Benedick. When I do name him, let it be thy part To praise him more than ever man did merit. My talk to thee must be how Benedick Is sick in love with Beatrice. (*No Fear*: 3.1.15–21)	*Hero and Ursula will talk about how much Benedick loves Beatrice and how wonderful he is. Hero will praise him extensively to help convince Beatrice.*	*She is a romantic because she wants to fix up her cousin with a partner.*
Claudio In mine eye she is the sweetest lady that ever I looked on. (*No Fear*: 1.1.146)	*Claudio thinks Hero is the most wonderful woman he has ever met.*	*Hero is appealing.*

*spark*teach   **77**

Text About Hero	What Text Says	What Text Reveals About Hero

Now review what you've recorded in column 3 about Hero's traits. Based on this list, do you think it makes sense that Hero did not speak up at the wedding and defend herself? Explain.

Elements of Comedy

Overview

Shakespeare's plays are divided into categories—comedy, tragedy, and history—and each type of drama has specific elements. Take a moment to review the definition and characteristics of Shakespeare's comedies with students. Then have students use this worksheet to find and list the comic elements in *Much Ado About Nothing*. Finally, have students respond to the prompt, taking a position as to whether the play actually is a Shakespearean tragicomedy. Students can write responses or discuss the prompt in small groups or as a class. Pass out this worksheet before students begin reading the play.

RL.11-12.1 Cite strong and thorough textual evidence to support analysis of what the text says explicitly as well as inferences drawn from the text, including determining where the text leaves matters uncertain.

RL.11-12.3 Analyze the impact of the author's choices regarding how to develop and relate elements of a story or drama (e.g., where a story is set, how the action is ordered, how the characters are introduced and developed).

RL.11-12.5 Analyze the impact of the author's choices regarding how to develop and relate elements of a story or drama (e.g., where a story is set, how the action is ordered, how the characters are introduced and developed).

SL.11-12.1 Initiate and participate effectively in a range of collaborative discussions (one-on-one, in groups, and teacher-led) with diverse partners on grades 11–12 topics, texts, and issues, building on others' ideas and expressing their own clearly and persuasively.

Elements of Comedy

Although today the comedy genre can refer to any piece of art that is funny, a comedy written by William Shakespeare contained specific elements. In brief, a comedy is one of Shakespeare's dramatic works that has an amusing tone, creates comic effects, and generally ends well. Shakespeare's language in a comedy creates a lighthearted tone and features wordplay, puns, and figurative speech. The plot revolves around misconceptions and deceptions, the struggles of young lovers, and mistaken identities or characters in disguise. The happy ending involves a wedding.

As you read *Much Ado About Nothing*, note down the elements that reveal that the play is a comedy. After finishing the play and completing the chart, respond to the prompt that follows.

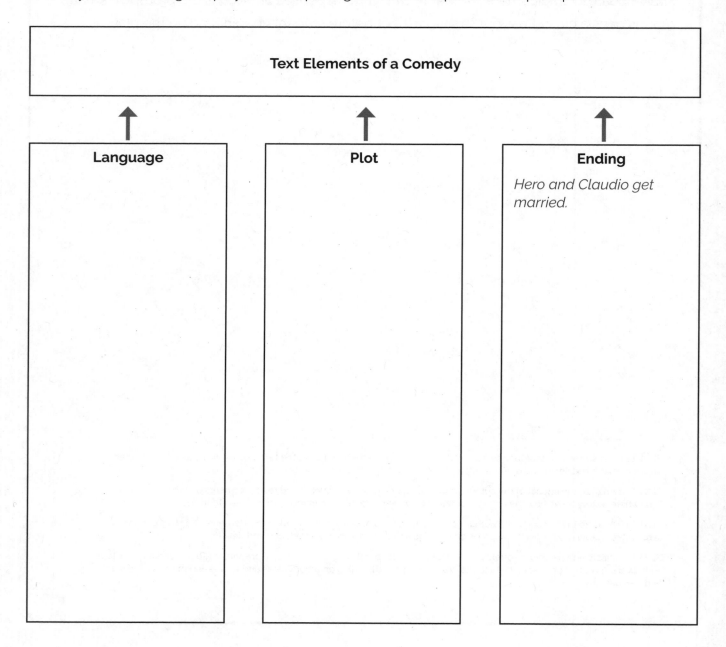

Text Elements of a Comedy

Language	**Plot**	**Ending**
		Hero and Claudio get married.

Prompt

A tragicomedy is a play that makes use of elements from both comedies and tragedies (which are serious plays with unhappy endings). For instance, a tragicomedy could be a serious play with funny moments or a happy ending, or a comic play that ends in the characters' deaths. Do you think *Much Ado About Nothing* is a tragicomedy? Discuss this idea, citing specific parts of the text to support your answer.

"The Merry War of Wits"

Overview

Readers cannot truly appreciate *Much Ado About Nothing* without having an understanding of the extravagant and clever wordplay Shakespeare puts in the mouths of his combative lovers, Beatrice and Benedick. Students will use this worksheet to closely read a scene that has been annotated to explain different types of wordplay typically found in the play and then review and annotate two other scenes on their own. In order to comprehend more wordplay throughout the play, this worksheet is best completed after reading Act 1, scene 1.

RL.11-12.4 Determine the meaning of words and phrases as they are used in the text, including figurative and connotative meanings; analyze the impact of specific word choices on meaning and tone, including words with multiple meanings or language that is particularly fresh, engaging, or beautiful. (Include Shakespeare as well as other authors.)

RL.11–12.6 Analyze a case in which grasping a point of view requires distinguishing what is directly stated in a text from what is really meant (e.g., satire, sarcasm, irony, or understatement).

SL.11-12.3 Evaluate a speaker's point of view, reasoning, and use of evidence and rhetoric, assessing the stance, premises, links among ideas, word choice, points of emphasis, and tone used.

W.11–12.3 Write narratives to develop real or imagined experiences or events using effective technique, well-chosen details, and well-structured event sequences.

"The Merry War of Wits"

From the moment they appear on stage, Beatrice and Benedick engage in verbal wordplay—both with one another and with others—that shows off their quick minds and quick tongues. Wordplay in *Much Ado About Nothing* takes many forms. Characters use sarcasm and repetition, insult one another, make jokes, play off each other's words with puns and intentional double meanings, and create lively metaphors and similes.

In the chart is a section from *Much Ado About Nothing* that has been annotated to explain Beatrice's witty speech. Read the scene and study the annotations to understand how Shakespeare employs wordplay.

Then create two charts in your notebook to annotate two more scenes: Beatrice and Benedick's meeting (*No Fear*: 1.1.93–114) and Claudio and Benedick discussing Hero (*No Fear*: 1.1.126–159). Annotate each scene to explain Shakespeare's wordplay. Note that some terms will be unfamiliar, but an understanding of every single line of text is not necessary to enjoy the overall humor.

Original Text (*No Fear*: 1.1.25–75)	Annotation
Beatrice I pray you, is Signor **Mountanto** returned from the wars or no? **Messenger** I know none of that name, lady. There was none such in the army of any sort. **Leonato** What is he that you ask for, niece? **Hero** My cousin means Signor Benedick of Padua. **Messenger** O, he's returned; and as pleasant as ever he was.	Insult/sarcasm: Beatrice calls Benedick by a fencing term, *montanto*, to insult him with a foolish name. There is also implied sarcasm since she claims not to care about Benedick but is still asking about him.

Beatrice

He set up his bills here in Messina and challenged Cupid at the flight, and my uncle's Fool, reading the challenge, subscribed for Cupid, and challenged him at the bird-bolt. I pray you, how many hath he **killed** and eaten in these wars? But how many hath he **killed**? For indeed I promised to eat all of his **killing**.

Leonato

Faith, niece, you tax Signor Benedick too much, but he'll be meet with you, I doubt it not.

Messenger

He hath done good service, lady, in these wars.

Beatrice

You had musty victual, and he hath holp to eat it. He is a very **valiant trencherman**. He hath an excellent stomach.

Messenger

And a **good soldier too**, lady.

Beatrice

And a **good soldier to** a lady, but what is he to a lord?

Messenger

A lord to a lord, a man to a man, **stuffed** with all honorable virtues.

Beatrice

It is so indeed. He is no less than a **stuffed** man. But for the stuffing—well, we are all mortal.

Repetition: While Beatrice's story is obscure, she intentionally repeats the word to render Benedick ridiculous.

Sarcasm/pun: Beatrice is being sarcastic when she calls Benedick valiant, or brave. She also calls him a trencherman, which is a hearty eater and a person who sponges off others.

Double meaning: The Messenger means a good soldier *also*, but Beatrice pretends he means Benedick is a good soldier *compared to* a lady.

Pun: The Messenger uses *stuffed* to mean "filled," but Beatrice changes the meaning into a stuffed man, or a dummy.

Leonato

You must not, sir, mistake my niece. There is a kind of merry war betwixt Signor Benedick and her. They never meet but there's a skirmish of wit between them.

Beatrice

Alas, he gets nothing by that. **In our last conflict four of his five wits went halting off, and now is the whole man governed with one, so that if he have wit enough to keep himself warm, let him bear it for a difference between himself and his horse**, for it is all the wealth that he hath left to be known a reasonable creature. Who is his companion now? He hath every month a new sworn brother.

> Insult: Beatrice says that Benedick lacks his wits since she beat him in their last verbal sparring and now he is no smarter than his horse.

Messenger

Is't possible?

Beatrice

Very easily possible. He wears his faith but as the fashion of his hat; it ever changes with the next block.

Messenger

I see, lady, the gentleman is not **in your books**.

Beatrice

No. **An he were, I would burn my study.** But, I pray you, who is his companion? Is there no young squarer now that will make a voyage with him to the devil?

> Double meaning: The Messenger uses *in your books* to mean "in your opinion" but Beatrice takes him literally to refer to the books in a library that she would destroy as a way of ridding herself of Benedick.

Messenger

He is most in the company of the right noble Claudio.

Beatrice

O Lord, **he will hang upon him like a disease! He is sooner caught than the pestilence, and the taker runs presently mad**. God help the noble Claudio! If he have caught the Benedick, it will cost him a thousand pound ere a be cured.

> Simile: Beatrice likens Benedick to a disease that will infect Claudio and drive him insane.

Original Text (*No Fear*: 1.1.25–75)	Annotation
Messenger I will hold friends with you, lady. **Beatrice** Do, good friend. **Leonato** **You will never run mad, niece.** **Beatrice** **No, not till a hot January.** **Messenger** Don Pedro is approached.	Joke: Leonato means that Beatrice will never fall victim to Benedick's charms, and Beatrice agrees by making a joke out of a highly unlikely event.

Driving Questions

Driving Questions	Initial Answer	Final Answer
Does Don Pedro need to wear a disguise and pretend to be Claudio to woo Hero for his friend? Why can't Claudio woo her himself?	Text evidence:	Text evidence:
Why does Don Pedro decide that Beatrice and Benedick should fall in love with one another, and how does he propose to make this happen?	Text evidence:	Text evidence:
Don John resolves to play tricks to interfere in Hero and Claudio's relationship. What motivates Don John?	Text evidence:	Text evidence:
What tricks and lies does Don Pedro use to make Benedick believe that Beatrice loves him?	Text evidence:	Text evidence:

Driving Questions	Initial Answer	Final Answer
What tricks and lies does Hero use to make Beatrice believe that Benedick loves her?	Text evidence:	Text evidence:
What are the serious ramifications of the trick that Don John plays on Claudio regarding Hero?	Text evidence:	Text evidence:
What is the lie the friar suggests telling about Hero? How does he expect the lie will uncover the truth and clear Hero's good name?	Text evidence:	Text evidence:
How does the wedding scene rely on tricks and lies?	Text evidence:	Text evidence:

The Path of True Love

The path of true love rarely runs smooth in the works of William Shakespeare, and *Much Ado About Nothing* presents no exception. The play focuses on two sets of lovers who are manipulated through trickery and lies—not just by their enemies, but by their friends and family as well. Use this worksheet to organize the chain of events that lead to a potential love connection between Beatrice and Benedick and a potential separation of Hero and Claudio. Write down the key events that help each plot unfold. Highlight the specific tricks and lies, their friends' and family's reactions, and the next moves forward. Be sure to include text citations. You may add additional boxes as needed.

The Beatrice and Benedick Plot

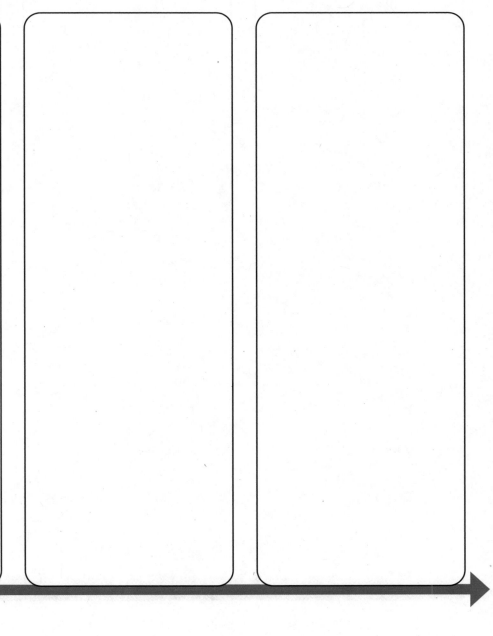

Don Pedro declares he has a way to trick Beatrice and Benedick into falling in love. Claudio and Hero agree to help. They go with Don Pedro to hear his plan.

(No Fear: 2.1.303–325)

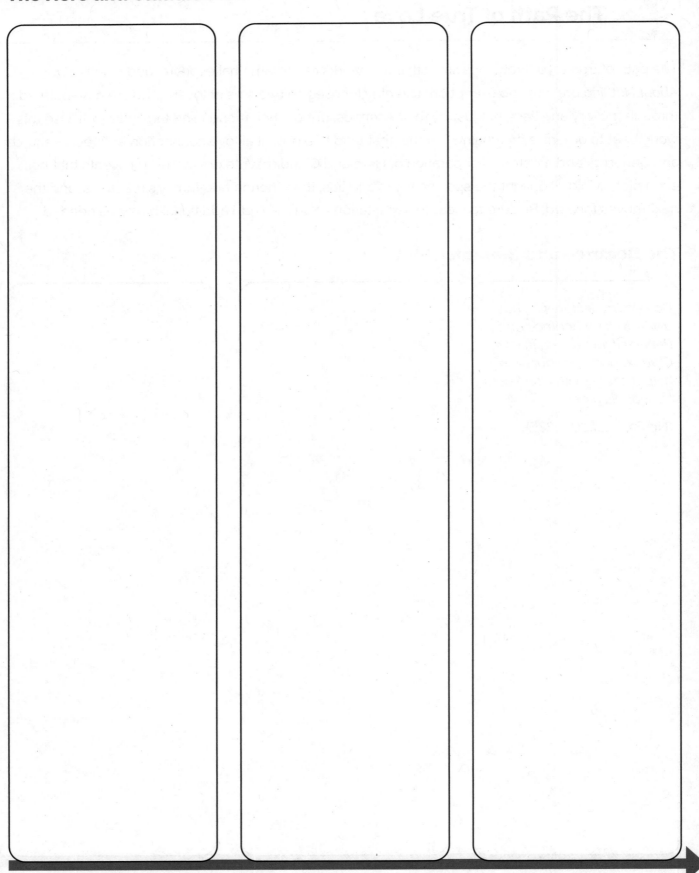

Prose in the Play

1. Define *prose*:

2. Read the following excerpt from *Much Ado About Nothing*. Identify it as prose or verse, and explain how you know.

BENEDICK

A miracle! Here's our own hands against our hearts. Come,

I will have thee, but, by this light, I take thee for pity.

BEATRICE

I would not deny you, but by this good day, I yield upon

great persuasion, and partly to save your life, for I was told

you were in a consumption.

(*No Fear*: 5.4.95–99)

3. Would Shakespeare likely represent a speech in which Hero explains how she feels about her marriage in prose or verse? Explain.

*spark*teach   **91**

4. Would Shakespeare likely represent a speech in which Beatrice describes a party she attended in prose or verse? Explain.

5. Find a piece of text (not from *Much Ado About Nothing*) written in prose. Explain why it is written in prose and why that is significant.

Through the Directors' Eyes

Answer Key

Sample Student Response

Branagh's Version	Whedon's Version
filmed in color	filmed in black and white
period setting and costumes	contemporary setting and costumes
smooth camera	handheld camera
includes Beatrice, Benedick and his entourage, and Leonato's household	includes only Beatrice and Benedick
camera mostly switches between Beatrice and Benedick	camera mostly frames both characters at the same time
film seems upbeat and playful	film seems somewhat serious and somber

RL.11-12.7 Analyze multiple interpretations of a story, drama, or poem (e.g., recorded or live production of a play or recorded novel or poetry), evaluating how each version interprets the source text. (Include at least one play by Shakespeare and one play by an American dramatist.)

Through the Directors' Eyes

Fill in the chart to show how each director presents key aspects of his movie. Consider elements such as setting, costume, characters, film and camera techniques, and any other parts of the scene that strike you. Add more rows as needed.

Branagh's Version	Whedon's Version
filmed in color	*filmed in black and white*

1. What aspects of Branagh's and Whedon's films are most like those of Shakespeare's play?

    Both films stick strictly to Shakespeare's words.

2. What aspects of Branagh's and Whedon's films differ the most from those of Shakespeare's play?

3. What is the overall mood of each scene? Which mood captures what you imagined when you first read the play?

4. Which movie do you think remains truest to the play? Which movie do you think represents the spirit of the relationship between Beatrice and Benedick most clearly? Are these the same?

5. Which movie scene did you enjoy the most? Explain.

*sparkteach

PART 4

Postmortem

After the unit, use the following Rubric for Student Assessment to assess your students' learning and the Student and Teacher Reflection worksheets to capture your experience with the Lesson Plans.

Rubric for Student Assessment

Overview

Using a rubric can help you assess students' learning more accurately and more consistently. Giving the rubric to your students before they begin a task that will be assessed also makes your expectations clear and encourages students to take responsibility for their own learning and success on an assignment. This rubric can be used across multiple midpoint activities and final projects to assess students' learning and understanding. You can also edit a version of the rubric to tailor it to specific learning goals you have for your classes.

Rubric for Student Assessment

Area of Performance	4	3	2	1
Content development	Work clearly and thoroughly addresses the prompt. All details/ideas support the main topic. Ideas are original, creative, and supported by numerous concrete details from the text.	Work mostly addresses the prompt. Most details/ideas support the main topic. A few concrete details from the text are provided.	Work doesn't stay on target and/or doesn't follow the prompt. Only a few supporting details are provided.	Work doesn't stay on target or follow the prompt. Ideas are confusing. Details are irrelevant or missing.
Organization	Details are presented in a logical and meaningful order. Essays or presentations include a clear introduction, body, and conclusion. Statements reflect critical thinking skills. Appropriate transitions are used to connect ideas.	Most details are presented in a logical order and are related to the main topic. The writing is clear, but the introduction, body, or conclusion needs strengthening.	Many details are presented in an illogical order or are unrelated to the main topic. The writing lacks a clear introduction, well-organized body, or a strong conclusion.	Details and ideas are poorly organized and unrelated to main topic.
Language and style	Writing or spoken language is smooth, coherent, and stays on topic. Sentence structure varies. Strong verbs and descriptive details and language clarify and strengthen ideas.	Writing or spoken language stays on topic but sentence structure doesn't vary. Some descriptive details are used to clarify ideas.	Some writing or spoken language doesn't flow and/or lacks creativity. Some language unrelated to or inappropriate for the main topic is used.	Writing or spoken language is confusing. Incomplete or run-on sentences are used. Many terms used are unrelated to or inappropriate for the main topic.

Area of Performance	4	3	2	1
Mechanics (when applicable)	All grammar and punctuation is correct. The writing is free of spelling errors.	The writing is mostly free of grammatical, mechanical, and spelling errors.	Writing contains several grammatical, punctuation, and spelling errors.	The writing contains numerous errors that make it difficult to understand.
Collaboration (when applicable)	Student played a valuable role in group work. Student worked well with others, listened respectfully to others' ideas, and resolved any challenges in an appropriate manner.	Student played an important role in group work but could have been more open to others' ideas and/or could have resolved challenges in a more constructive manner.	Student did minimal work in his/her group. Student ignored group challenges or left challenges unresolved.	Student didn't do her/his fair share of work. Student did not engage in the group task.
Research (when applicable)	Multiple, reliable sources were used to gather information. All sources are properly cited or credited.	Some research was done to complete the task. Not all sources are cited or some citations are incomplete.	Little or no research was done to gather necessary information. No sources are cited.	No research was done.

Student and Teacher Reflection Worksheets

Overview

A reflective practice helps you continue to develop new and engaging teaching strategies that meet the needs of all students in your class. Tracking successes as well as challenges throughout a unit of study also decreases planning time for future classes and helps you tailor your lessons to improve each time you teach them. Use this worksheet to reflect on a Real-Life Lens Lesson you have taught and record what was successful and what you would change when you teach the material again. Make notes on interesting ideas you added to the Lens Lesson or thoughts your students had that inspired you along the way.

Student Reflection Worksheet

1. How did reading the text through the lens of tricks and lies affect your engagement with and understanding of this text?

   _____

   _____

   _____

2. What difficulties did you encounter with this text, and how did you address them?

   _____

   _____

   _____

3. Consider the Real-Life Links you encountered at the beginning of the lesson. Which resources did you find the most interesting? Why?

   _____

   _____

4. How effective were the Driving Questions in guiding you to a deeper understanding of the text?

   _____

   _____

   _____

5. Describe one challenge you faced while working on an activity or project and how you overcame it.

   _____

   _____

   _____

6. What new insight or skill did you take away from this lesson?

   _____

   _____

   _____

Teacher Reflection Worksheet

1. How did the lens applied in this lesson affect student engagement and comprehension?

_____

_____

_____

2. How did students respond to the Real-Life Links? Did some resources spark more interest than others?

_____

_____

_____

3. Did you or any of your students come up with additional Driving Questions? If so, record them here to use the next time you teach this lesson.

_____

_____

4. Which activities inspired students the most?

_____

_____

_____

5. What difficulties did students encounter, how did you address them, and were your interventions successful?

_____

_____

_____

6. Were there worksheets, activities, or projects that you will revise the next time you present this lesson? If so, what changes will you make?

_____

_____

_____

Notes

Notes

Notes

Notes

Notes